Clifford K. Berryman
1869-1949

This sketch of Clifford K. Berryman at his drawing board was drawn by his son, James T. Berryman. There are several generations of Washingtonians who came to know and love Clifford Berryman through is cartoons. He had the faculty of achieving the sort of satire that never left a scar. The memory of Clifford Berryman will live on through his drawings, but most of all he will long be remembered by his creation of the little bear, the likeness of which will live on forever in thousands of toy reproductions. *Courtesy Smithsonian Institution.*

The evolution of our little friend the Teddy Bear is only one of the many events in Theodore Roosevelt's life we must honor him for. He was one of the greatest statesmen in the country and the youngest President of the United States. *Artwork by Murray Harris.*

The Teddy Bear Men:

Theodore Roosevelt & Clifford Berryman

by Linda Mullins

Published By 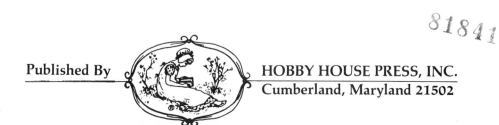 HOBBY HOUSE PRESS, INC.
Cumberland, Maryland 21502

Dedication

In memory of my gracious and loving mother.

Personal Acknowledgments

I wish to extend by sincere thanks and appreciation to Florence Berryman for sharing with me personal memories of her beloved father, to the Berryman family for allowing me to include photographs of their Uncle Cliff's original work from their collections and to Gregory Joseph for first introducing me to a member of the Berryman family.

To my very special friend, Georgi Bohrod Rothe, whose support and insight is particularly important to me. My sincere gratitude goes out to Mary Ternes who found time in her busy schedule as photo librarian at the District of Columbia Public Library, to help me with my research at the Library of Congress; to Evelyn Gathings for her fine artwork; and to Sandra Desmonde for her contribution of information on Roosevelt's Mississippi Bear Hunt.

A special thank you to my publisher, Gary R. Ruddell, for making this book possible, and to my editor, Virginia Ann Heyerdahl, for her invaluable advice and patience.

Most of all, to my patient and supportive husband, Wally, who often wonders what he ever got himself into when he gave me my first antique Teddy Bear.

Front Cover: Theodore Roosevelt in his Rough Rider uniform with his arm affectionately around Clifford Berryman's famous cartoon symbol — The Teddy Bear. **Courtesy Library of Congress.** (The color added to Berryman's cartoon is an artist's interpretation by Pam Baker.)

Additional copies of this book may be purchased at $12.95

plus $1.75 postage/handling from

HOBBY HOUSE PRESS, INC.

900 Frederick Street, Cumberland, Maryland 21502

ISBN: 0-87588-308-7

Table of Contents

Acknowledgments

My gratitude to the following companies and organizations for their assistance.

American Stock Photos, Los Angeles, California.

Bettman Archives, New York, New York.

Charles Scribner's Sons, New York, New York.

Corcoran Gallery of Art, Washington, D.C.

District of Columbia Public Library, Washington, D.C. (Mary C. Ternes, photo librarian)

Eastern National Parks and Monuments Association, Philadelphia, Pennsylvania.

Geyer-McAllister Publications, *Playthings*, New York, New York.

Library of Congress, Washington, D.C.

Manhattan Sites National Park Service, (Diane Duszak).

New York Historical Society, New York, New York.

Old Court House Museum, Vicksburg, Mississippi, (Gordon A. Cotton, director).

Smithsonian Institution, Washington, D.C., (Division of Political History, William L. Bird, Jr.).

Southern States Images, Jackson, Mississippi, (Don Gaddis).

Theodore Roosevelt Collection, Harvard Library, (Wallace F. Daily, curator).

Time, New York, New York.

Margarete Steiff G.M.B.H., West Germany, (Dr. H. Zimmermann, president), (Jorg Junginger, [Steiff]).

Margaret Woodbury Strong Museum, Rochester, New York.

United States Department of Agriculture, Jackson, Mississippi.

University of Hartford, West Hartford, Connecticut, (Dr. Edmund Sullivan).

National Press Club, Washington, D.C., (Barbara P. Vandegrift, Librarian-archivist).

Thank you to the following collectors for sharing their collections with me.

Austin, Betty Berryman
Austin, Betty Ruth
Berryman, Florence
Eldridge, Ernie
Emory, Flore
Fraley, Tobin, Maurice and Nina
Friz, Richard
Gambil, Jan
Hake, Theodore
Harris, Chick
Harris, Murray and Bea
Hiscox, Mimi
Hogan, Beth Diane
Jorgensen, Fred
Kaonis, Keith and Donna
Lauver, Barbara
Mathies, Dr. and Mrs. Allen
Nicholson, Susan Brown
Port, Beverly
Roberts, Toby
Schoonmaker, Patricia N.
Sickler, Joan
Tisch, Shirley
Volpp, Paul and Rosemary
Waddell, Judith

Introduction

The story of the Teddy Bear's actual creator has caused considerable controversy over the years. A wealth of information has been uncovered and published in many wonderful books. However, when I began my research for my last book, *Teddy Bears Past and Present*, I found yet another part of Teddy's beginning that had different historical accounts.

It involved Clifford K. Berryman and President Theodore Roosevelt. Berryman was the political cartoonist who immortalized President Roosevelt's renowned 1902 bear hunt in his legendary cartoon "Drawing the Line in Mississippi."

It was this event that inspired me to make a trip to the Library of Congress in Washington, D.C., to try to uncover what really happened some 85 years ago. In addition to being able to uncover the real story, I found myself deeply involved with the lives of these two great men and their fascinating association with the Teddy Bear.

I have not attempted in this book to write a biography of Clifford Berryman and Theodore Roosevelt, but to include exciting highlights and numerous illustrations of their eventful lives as they pertain to the interest of Arctophilists (bear lovers).

Chapter One

The Life Of Clifford K. Berryman

For half a century Clifford Kennedy Berryman was the nation's most famous and beloved political graphic commentator.

His drawings are historical literature, recording events through the years in pictures instead of words.

Unlike many of his predecessors who showed no restraint, he brought to his profession a gentle touch. Berryman's drawings were never mean nor vindictive. His zest for living and sparkling wit was transmitted in his cartoons.

Mr. Berryman's romantic story is of a small town boy who worked his way to Washington to become one of the best known cartoonists in American history.

Born on April 2, 1869, near Versailles, Kentucky, in the tiny village of Clifton, on the Kentucky River, Clifford Kennedy Berryman was the tenth among the 11 children of James T. and Sally Church Berryman.

As far as art was concerned he never took a drawing lesson in his life. He inherited the talent from his English-Scottish father, a planter and merchant, who owned a country store in Versailles. To entertain his children, he demonstrated his artistry, by caricaturing his rural neighbors and customers on wrapping paper as a hobby. To his son's everlasting disappointment, these sketches were not preserved.

Clifford's father died at the age of 57. Clifford was only ten. Berryman's early youth was delightfully eventful.

He received his first recognition in the field of art when he drew a chalk portrait of his teacher on the blackboard of the little log cabin schoolhouse (*Illustration 1*). Although the true likeness of the sketch delighted his fellow classmates, his teacher unfortunately did not share their appreciation. In fact, his action was so unfavorable that the young artist found it more comfortable to take his lessons in a standing position for the next few days.

At the age of ten, he narrowly escaped being gored to death by a supposedly friendly cow he attempted to sketch.

Berryman would tell the humorous but true tale of a childhood incident that influenced his preference for a pencil over a brush:

"When I was a boy down in Kentucky, my father always kept a large can of shoe blacking just outside the back door, and attached was a dauber.

"One year, when I was a little lad, our house had just been repainted — a fresh, glistening white. Somehow that snowy paint fascinated

Illustration 1. Clifford Berryman first received recognition in the field of art when he drew a chalk portrait of his teacher on the blackboard of the little log cabin schoolhouse. Unfortunately, his teacher did not share the same appreciation as his classmates. *Artwork by Evelyn Gathings.*

Washington. D.C. April 12th. 1890.

My dear Mother:

Today, 68 years ago, my father came into this world, and I can hardly believe that he would be nearly seventy years of age if he were living. The 12th of this month is a day that I never allow to go by unnoticed and I know you never allow it to escape your memory. I often wonder why it was that he was called away just in the prime of life, but I suppose it is one of the things that "we shall know hereafter". I do know one thing now and that is, that no boys ever had a father (or no woman ever had a husband) that they could be more proud of than we boys and you. If I can only be half of the man, that my father was, I surely can ask no more. None of his sons will ever be the man that James T. Berryman was. I have often heard people make that remark and it is a very true one!

Illustration 2. This pen sketch Clifford Berryman drew of his father, in a letter he sentimentally wrote to his mother just after he moved to Washington (April 12, 1890), is an early example of his natural talent for sketching a true likeness in an almost photographic style. *Courtesy Library of Congress.*

Illustration 3. Clifford K. Berryman was a very distinguished, handsome young artist. *Courtesy Florence Berryman.*

cigar box so it would stand up. His Uncle Ed liked it so well he kept it in a prominent place on his desk.

It was a few years later (when Cliff was 17) before Blackburn (now Senator) saw the likeness by chance in Clifford's uncle's office, a two-story brick house located on Morgan Street. Overwhelmed by the young artist's ability to draw he asked:

"Where did you get that statue of me, Ed?"

"One of Jim's boys made it," said Uncle Ed.

"Where is he now?" asked the great man.

"Down on the Kentucky River, on their farm."

"That boy's got talent," said the Senator, "I'm going to take him to Washington and see what I can do for him."

Senator Blackburn was true to his word. He arranged a position for Clifford as a draftsman. The young man was paid $30 per month for his work in the Patent Office. The striving young artist borrowed $100 from his brother to enable him to buy his railroad fare and a new suit.

After his graduation at 17, he arrived in Washington on August 4, 1886. He wore his overcoat in the belief that the nation's capital was far north of Kentucky, towards the Arctic Circle (Cliff had never been farther than 55 miles from his house until then) and was bound to be cold.

The first few months of his salary were used up by paying $20 for his room and board and $10 for repaying his debt.

However, Berryman remembers those early years of hardship as being happy ones. At the Patent Office he used his first bottle of real drawing ink, but he took to it "like a duck to water."

The young protégé of Senator Blackburn amused himself at night by humorously sketching the community habits of Capitol Hill. He worked hard improving his skills by studying and copying the drawings of the foremost caricaturists and cartoonists represented in such contemporary periodicals as *Puck*, *Punch* and *Judge*.

He progressed at the Patent Office to freehand illustration of subjects submitted for patent protection, and in this position he received a $10 a month raise.

He celebrated by opening a savings account and began courting Miss Kate G. Durfee, a Washington girl, who became Mrs. Clifford Berryman in 1893 (for information on Clifford's wife, please refer to Chapter Twelve, "Mrs. Berryman and Her Testimonial at Her Husband's 80th Birthday Party"). Later they became the proud parents of three children: Mary Belle, Florence Seville and James Thomas. Only Florence Berryman is living (for information on the children, please refer to Chapter Thirteen, "The Children of Clifford Berryman").

His progress as an eager student of the political scene during those early years led to a major breakthrough in his career in 1891.

me, and I decided to investigate the artistic effects that might be produced on it with a blacking brush.

"When my father saw the results, I received a good sound spanking. As a result, I never had any use for brushes after that...I've always worked with a pen."

"Cliff," as his friends knew him, attended Professor Henry's School for Boys, a private academy from which he graduated when he was 17. He paid for his tuition by driving the Clifton mail wagon, carrying the mail to and from Versailles for two years. He soon combined his early enthusiasm and talents for drawing, with an eager interest in politics. This combination later developed into his life's work.

At 13 he had a strong admiration for Representative (later Senator) Joseph C. S. Blackburn, described as a "chivalrous and gallant" man. Young Berryman played hooky from school to listen to his idol's campaign speech. So impressed was the boy by the Congressman that when he returned, he drew a sketch of his hero.

Cutting out the silhouette with a jigsaw he had purchased for $1.00 from his earnings as a clerk in the country store, he then mounted the picture on top of a

He apprehensively submitted some drawings of a picnic at Marshall Hall to Frank Hatton, who, with Beriah Wilkins, then owned *The Washington Post*.

To his delight, *The Post* published them. He said he was afraid to go near the paper for a few days after that — afraid they would charge him advertising rates for the space, but instead they paid the shy young artist $25, only $5 less than he was making a month at the Patent Office.

From 1891 to 1896 he earned his living and gained his reputation as a general illustrator. Those years made him more self-assured and brought him in touch with the public.

In 1896 he was employed full time for *The Washington Post* and worked as George Y. Coffin's editorial (cartoonist) understudy. When Coffin died in 1896, Berryman became his successor, working for seven years in the style he had learned from his predecessor, "never coarse, never brutal, never malignant."

In those days the camera was not used much in the newspaper business, so Mr. Berryman did all his drawings from real life. He developed the ability for sketching a true likeness in an almost photographic style that was easily recognized.

It was during his service with *The Washington Post* that Berryman created what was probably the most popular of all cartoon symbols, and the one with whom we still associate him — his little Berryman Bear, or, as it is better known to us, the "Teddy Bear."

The little bear came into being after news of President Theodore Roosevelt's refusal to shoot a defenseless captured bear during a Mississippi bear hunt reached Berryman at *The Washington Post* (for information on the hunt, please refer to Chapter Three, "The Real Story of Theodore Roosevelt's 1902 Mississippi Bear Hunt").

The imaginative artist depicted this sportsmanlike incident on the front page as part of a montage titled "The Passing Show" on November 16, 1902 (*Illustration 5*). Apparently having in mind the race riots which had occurred shortly before in Brownsville, Texas, he gave the cartoon the title "Drawing the Line in Mississippi" (for information on the cartoon, please refer to Chapter Two, "The Mystery of the Two Berryman Cartoons —'Drawing the Line in Mississippi' ").

The public response was overwhelming. Berryman received floods of letters requesting "repeats" of the bear.

As a result of this inspirational drawing, the bear became his "dingbat" (cartoonist symbol). (For information on the symbol, please refer to Chapter Four, "The Development of Clifford Berryman's Famous Cartoon Symbol — The Teddy Bear.")

Because of the association with Theodore Roosevelt, the popular little bear began to make regular appearances whenever Berryman drew the President.

During those early years with *The Washington Post*, Berryman's cartoons recorded a variety of notable

Illustration 4. Rendering of the Berryman Coat of Arms. The name Berryman is traced to the French province of Berri, France. The 14th century Duc de Berri was a patron of the arts who employed the finest medieval miniature painters yet known.

Some of his descendants migrated to England very early. In the 16th century John de Berri of Upcott, England, anglicized his name to Berryman. In 1654 his great-grandson, John, (and his wife Elizabeth) came to America and settled in Westmoreland County, Virginia.

Several centuries earlier, Normans under William the Conqueror had many descendants, among them the 25 barons of Runnemede, who forced King John in 1254 to sign the Magna Carta.

From the 17th century on, Clifford Berryman's ancestors were all English and Scottish and settled in Virginia and later Kentucky. *Information courtesy Florence Berryman. Photograph courtesy Betty Ruth Austin.*

events from the Spanish-American War to the discovery of the North Pole.

Clifford left *The Washington Post* after he had become their chief cartoonist, to fulfill his long ambition to work for *The Washington Evening Star*.

He joined the staff of *The Evening Star* in 1907, succeeding Mr. Felix Mahoney. He took with him, of course, his trademark, the lovable little creature that was now internationally famous — the Teddy Bear.

Illustration 5. On November 16, 1902, Clifford K. Berryman depicted President Theodore Roosevelt's refusal to shoot a captured bear during a 1902 Mississippi bear hunt on page one of *The Washington Post* as part of a montage titled "The Passing Show." Berryman's famous cartoon symbol originated from this drawing. *Courtesy Library of Congress.*

The first cartoon Berryman drew for *The Evening Star* was on January 31, 1907. It was of President Theodore Roosevelt's historic declaration that he would not be a candidate in the 1908 campaign. In the bottom left-hand corner of the cartoon, making his debut appearance, was Berryman's bear, looking happy about his new position and introducing himself by shaking hands with *The Star* (Illustration 19).

For more than 30 years Berryman's cartoons in *The Evening Star* commented on the news every day, seven days a week. This is believed to be a record among American cartoonists.

This enthusiastic and energetic man was loved by his colleagues for himself and for his inspiring loyalty that marked his long years of service. During his career, Berryman's cartoons were an integral part of *The Evening Star*, but his contributions went beyond that.

He was called "The Dean of the American Cartoonists," "one of the most thoughtful and constructive political philosophers of his day" and the "pride and boast of the city of Washington." He earned his reputation of achieving the sort of "satire that never left a scar." His cartoons were so to the point that even those who suffered from his pen always agreed with the moral of his drawing.

A country boy at heart, he was admired for his sensitive and genuine personality.

Berryman never forgot the advice he received from his editor, Crosby S. Noyes, early in his career on *The Evening Star*. The cartoonist was concerned one of his drawings was too harsh, and asked for the experienced comments of the editor, who told him: "To be on the safe side whenever any doubt arises about one of your cartoons throw it into the waste basket. Take some other idea."

Clifford Berryman probably had a wider circle of acquaintances in Washington then any other private citizen. He was an intimate friend of Mark Twain, and knew every president of the United States from Grover Cleveland to Harry Truman. He played golf with them and was their guest in the Presidential Box at baseball games. He received letters of appreciation from Theodore Roosevelt and each Chief Executive of his time.

Although Berryman was a busy prominent figure in Washington, he always had time for his friends and associates. Many a young boy in his teens, aspiring to be a cartoonist, came to Mr. Berryman seeking his valued advice. The vigorous and dedicated cartoonist crammed as much as he could into his life.

He used the streetcar or bus each day to go to the office because he felt it gave him an insight into human nature. He never worked at home, but would spend hours in his "cubbyhole" (as he called his office), which was piled high with old newspapers and drawings. He would read the newspapers searching for ideas, sketching as he read. A subject and event chosen, he would then meet with the editor to discuss his concept. With the editor's approval he then hastily returned to his drafting board to produce his cartoon.

Illustration 6. Because of the association with Theodore Roosevelt, the popular little bear began to make regular appearances whenever Berryman drew the President. "The President and the Hospitable South," *The Washington Post*, from the book *A Cartoon History of Roosevelt's Career* by Albert Shaw, copyright 1910 by The Review of Reviews Company. *Courtesy Toby Roberts.*

Illustration 7. "Presidential Tug Don't Spatter the Boat T.R." After the historical hunt, in almost every cartoon with Roosevelt, the mischievous little Teddy Bear could be seen "helping out" his new friend, the President. November 6, 1904 (?). *Courtesy Smithsonian Institution.*

Illustration 8. "Wanted Pruning Shears." The little bear always appears to have his nose into whatever President Roosevelt is doing. *Courtesy Smithsonian Institution.*

Illustration 9. "President Roosevelt being Welcomed to Dixie Land," *The Washington Post,* from the book *A Cartoon History of Roosevelt's Career* by Albert Shaw, copyright 1910 by The Review of Reviews Company. *Courtesy Toby Roberts.*

Illustration 10. "The President and Secretary Hitchcock are after Big Game in the Public Lands of the Northwest," *The Washington Post*, from the book *A Cartoon History of Roosevelt's Career* by Albert Shaw, copyright 1910 by The Review of Reviews Company. *Courtesy Toby Roberts.*

Illustration 11. During my visit to the Smithsonian National Museum of History and Technology, I placed my request for copies of the Berryman cartoons for reproduction in my book from the originals in the collection. Due to the cartoons being drawn on perishable material, the collection is preserved in storage and only displayed for specific exhibits. This also applies to the collection of Berryman cartoons at the Corcoran Gallery of Art.

Illustration 12. This cartoon from the collection of the Smithsonian National Museum of History and Technology is one of my favorite drawings of Berryman's Teddy Bear. The little cartoon character earned the reputation of representing all that was good in the world. Original. *Courtesy Smithsonian Institution.*

Illustration 13. "What the President Hopes to Find," *The Evening Star*, December 27, 1907. *Courtesy Library of Congress.*

Illustration 14. The little Teddy Bear looks horrified as he peers in the trunk full of bear skins that arrived for the President. *Courtesy Theodore Roosevelt Collection, Harvard College Library.*

Illustration 15. "Specials Today" inscribed to C. Cory Campbell, a cartoonist who usually favored Democrats in his cartoons. They are the "Hard Bunch" Berryman refers to in his inscription. Original. *Courtesy The University of Hartford.*

Illustration 16. Teddy Roosevelt riding a Wyoming horse rounding up steers labeled as states. *Courtesy Library of Congress.*

Berryman worked solely in pen and ink. He never believed in using mechanical aids for drawing. His pen alone was his professional instrument.

He loved to draw and would approach each cartoon as if it were a new adventure. Even though his cartoons were not required for publication until the following day, he would expedite each drawing as if he was working on a deadline for the next edition.

As soon as he finished his drawing (he was known to produce a cartoon in less than a half hour), he would rush out to show it to the first person he came upon to see their reaction.

Berryman allowed no substitutions for his cartoons. Even when he made a trip to Europe with Mrs. Berryman he drew 50 cartoons before he left. It was not until he became ill in 1934 and required surgery that he permitted his son James to take his place.

James, who had inherited his father's talent and style, was *The Washington Evening Star* daily sports cartoonist (for information on James Berryman, please refer to Chapter Thirteen, "The Children of Clifford K. Berryman").

Throughout his eventful life, Clifford Berryman drew more than 15,000 cartoons. Of all those thousands

THE PRESIDENT'S DREAM.

Illustration 17. With the popularity of Teddy Bears and the derivation of their name from President Roosevelt's nickname "Teddy" many of Clifford Berryman's cartoons depicted bears. *Courtesy Theodore Roosevelt Collection, Harvard College Library.*

of people he cartooned not one ever complained that his feelings had been hurt. Berryman never commercialized any of his art. He loved his profession, and did not draw for money. When asked about his salary early in his career, he said, "It is enough to keep the back door shut on the wolf, anyway and I can watch the front door."

His only source of profit was his position as chief cartoonist of *The Evening Star* and his profits from illustrating over 37 books.

During his career his cartoons were in great demand. It became a tradition that the "victims" of his pen were the first to ask for the originals, and Berryman always

acceded generously. He literally gave away thousands of drawings.

One of his most ardent admirers was President Truman, whose office walls were said to have been adorned with many samples of his work.

In a congratulatory letter honoring Berryman's 80th birthday, President Truman wrote:

"To me you are ageless and timeless. You are a Washington institution comparable to the Monument. Presidents, Senators and even Supreme Court Justices come and go, but the Monument and Berryman stand.

Illustration 18. An *Evening Star* cartoonist illustrated an article "Berryman Bear Man" on January 24, 1907. Depicting Clifford Berryman with his famous bear, the article introduced the readers to Berryman, who was to join *The Evening Star* the following week. *Courtesy Library of Congress.*

"Though absent in flesh, I am with you in spirit, and I trust that your chairman will let me propose a toast — 'To Cliff Berryman, scholar and gentleman friend of humanity cartoonist extraordinary!' "

· Though there are notable small collections (for information of locations of collections, please see listing, "Locations of Clifford K. Berryman's Cartoon Collections"), many original drawings are owned by individuals. Perhaps the honor which Clifford Berryman regarded as the highest of his career was when the Librarian of Congress, Archibald MacLeish, requested that his original drawings be permanently placed in the Library's Cabinet of American Illustration, a division in which the leading illustrators of America are represented.

On January 19, 1945, he gave his gift to the Library of Congress. "My best work for half a century," he said, "is here. You will find the drawings just as they went to the engraver and they appeared in *The Evening Star*." It is believed the Berryman archives contain some 5000 sketches.

Illustration 19. The first cartoon Clifford Berryman drew for *The Washington Evening Star* was on January 31, 1907. It was of President Theodore Roosevelt's historic declaration that he would not be a candidate in the 1908 campaign. All the possible presidential candidates were anxious to hear Mr. Roosevelt repeat his declaration of two years before, that he would not be a candidate for a third term. In the bottom left-hand corner of the cartoon, making his debut appearance was Berryman's bear looking happy about his new position as he introduces himself to *The Star*. *Courtesy Smithsonian Institution.*

Illustration 20. "Yes, We're Making No Appointments Today!" Original. *Courtesy Judith Waddell.*

Illustration 21. "Merry Christmas To All." Original. *Courtesy Judith Waddell.*

A Great Team of Star Cartoonists

Their Page One Pictures Made This Book

Illustration 22. The Great Team of Star Cartoonists as they were shown in *The Campaign of '48 in Star Cartoons* book. Clifford Berryman (center), who artistically cartooned the pictorial history of the Senate for several decades, also shared his experience and knowledge with his son Jim Berryman (left) and Gib Crockett (right). Both men were his collegues at *The Star. Courtesy Library of Congress.*

Illustration 23. Clifford Berryman, dean of *The Star's* cartoonists, chats with President Truman after presenting him with a handsomely bound collection of campaign cartoons. At the President's request, Mr. Berryman penned an autograph, complete with the traditional Teddy Bear. *Courtesy D.C. Public Library.*

Illustration 24. One of Clifford Berryman's own most treasured possessions was his collection of autographed pen portraits of famous men and women. Each signature was accompanied by a beautifully drawn pen and ink portrait of the subject. It was only appropriate that when Berryman received Theodore Roosevelt's signature, his friend the little Teddy Bear with whom he had become so historically associated, should appear on the page also. *Courtesy Library of Congress.*

The Library of Congress hopes many of the widespread cartoons will eventually find their way to the master collection. Other treasured pieces of his work were his letters, illustrated with unmistakable sketches of the recipients. His answers to invitations and society meetings are cherished pieces of his artwork.

He would draw his little Teddy Bear for the casual caller who asked for his autograph. His cartoons became highly sought-after works of art, but to the generous artist they were of no monetary value and he gave many of them away.

Clifford Berryman was a busy man but he always had time for people, continuously sharing his knowledge, ideas, drawings and talent. He was greatly in demand by charitable and art groups or for other causes.

Not only a gifted artist, Berryman was also a captivating speaker and his audiences were always interested in his story of how he first came to draw his famous cartoon symbol — the Teddy Bear.

He was well-known for his delightful "chalk-talks," illustrating these talks with fascinating sketches reviewing some of the most interesting features of his career. He would draw a series of cartoons about "Squash Center." These were rural characters he remembered from his youth who gathered around the stove in his father's country store, where he once measured the flour and sugar.

At the conclusion of his talks he would carelessly toss the completed sketches aside. Hastily his admirers would come forth from the audience trying to be the first to claim his work. On one occasion he was actually asked if he would handle his work with more care and if

possible, avoid stepping on the discarded sketches. He drew his figures life-size using a lithographic crayon on brown paper. He had a phenomenal memory and would capture his audience with stories as he drew the various men in public life, both past and present.

So in demand was the entertaining artist as a speaker that he was only able to accept a small percentage of the many invitations he would receive.

One of Berryman's own most treasured possessions was his collection of autographed pen portraits of famous men and women, probably the most interesting in existence. In 1898 he completed his first album with nearly 60 famous men and women of that year. Each signature was accompanied with a beautifully drawn pen portrait of the subject (*Illustration 24*). Several of the sketches were drawn after the signatures were obtained, while others were made ahead to entice the celebrities for their autograph. Some years after Clifford Berryman's death, his daughter, Florence, a retired art critic for *The Evening Star*, (for information on Florence Berryman, please refer to Chapter Thirteen, "The Children of Clifford K. Berryman") presented a collection of her father's books, correspondence and manuscripts to the Library of Congress. Included in the gift were two of Berryman's cherished autograph books, containing greetings to the famous cartoonist from every president from Cleveland to Eisenhower. This collection is presently located in the library's manuscript department.

In May 1944, Berryman won the Pulitzer Prize (award for distinguished example of a journalistic work) for his cartoon "But Where is the Boat Going" published in *The Evening Star* August 28, 1943. (His

Illustration 25. In May 1944, Clifford Berryman won the Pulitzer Prize (award for distinguished example of journalistic work) for his cartoon "But Where is the Boat Going," published in *The Washington Evening Star*, August 28, 1943. (His colleagues felt the recognition was rather belated.) *Courtesy Smithsonian Institution.*

colleagues felt the recognition was rather belated.) It presented the "manpower mobilization muddle," showing a crowded dinghy with seven sturdy male figures in sailor clothes. (*Illustration 25*).

A man of enthusiasm and numerous personal interests, Clifford Berryman was an active member of many clubs. His biography in *Who's Who* placed the Literary Society first on the list. He was the first cartoonist to become a member of the Gridiron Club (the most famous dining club in the world), organized by Washington correspondents. It has been stated the club's objective is "to prevent pompous persons from taking themselves too seriously."

During an informal dinner in 1942 when Berryman was the guest of honor, he reminisced about his first dinner he attended 35 years previously. Preceding

election into the society, he served a nine-year apprenticeship of friendly labor for the club by illustrating its menu cards.

On his initiation that evening he was escorted to the platform by two members dressed as Teddy Bears — a strange coincidence was that the man who inspired the drawing of Berryman's Bear sat at the head of the table that night — President Theodore Roosevelt.

Another amusing event was on the 41st anniversary of Berryman's Bear in 1943. A fete was given by the American Newspaper Women's Club in their attractive headquarters at 1604 Twentieth Street, where they hung the organization's first possession, an original drawing of "Teddy."

An attractive wood carving by Gibson M. Crockett depicting a Teddy Bear holding a sketching pen with an

Illustration 26. Jim Berryman, as a tribute to his father (Clifford Berryman) winning the Pulitzer Prize Award, drew this cartoon. Note Berryman's little bear perched on top of his drawing board, applauding his beloved creator. Jim would only draw the popular bear when cartooning his father. *The Evening Star*, May 2, 1944. *Courtesy Library of Congress.*

overturned inkwell at his feet mounted on an artist's drawing board was presented to their honored guest.

In his later years many senators honored Clifford Berryman on his birthdays by celebrations or letters of congratulations. At a luncheon in his honor for his 75th birthday attended by a group of 12 senators (*Illustration 36*), Colonel Halsey read a tribute in verse to Berryman's famous Teddy Bear:

"But the Teddy bear with the padded paw
And the crafty eye that looked and saw
And appeared in the pictures you were wont to draw
Sure packed a wallop with a velvety paw.

This Teddy bear is a fine little merry one
When drawn by the pen of C.K. Berryman!"

A number of presents were produced. Among them was a Teddy Bear wearing a very abbreviated skirt which, explained one of the senators, was shortened by rationing. President Franklin D. Roosevelt said in his congratulatory letter on the occasion of Berryman's 70th birthday: "You have imparted to life as to art, a light and deft touch. You have been unwearied in the quest for beauty while at the same time you have brought light into dark places and taught us the value of a smile."

The Corcoran Gallery of Art in Washington, D.C.,

Illustration 27. The bears surprise the President with a special greeting during his visit to Colorado. *Courtesy Theodore Roosevelt Collection, Harvard College Library.*

Illustration 28. "Presiding Over the Senate," *The Washington Post* from the book, *A Cartoon History of Roosevelt's Career* by Albert Shaw, copyright 1910 by The Review of Reviews Company. President Roosevelt was affectionately nicknamed "Teddy," the name he lent a special toy in the early 1900s — the Teddy Bear. *Courtesy Toby Roberts.*

opened an exhibition of more than 250 of Clifford Berryman's original cartoons on July 5th, 1943. *The Evening Star* cartoonist received double honors that day as he celebrated his 50th wedding anniversary.

Mr. Minnigerode, director of the gallery, paid tribute to the 74-year-old veteran cartoonist by saying:

"Mr. Berryman's cartoons are so well-known — not only in Washington, where they have been published daily in *The Evening Star* for many years, but throughout the country — that they need no introduction. They never fail to reflect the character and personality of the artist, and his gentle and tolerant attitude toward his fellow man. They are never unkind, never bitter; never hurt nor give justifiable offense, and never carry with them what may be termed a 'sting.' But they are invariably clever, always timely; possess a rare sense of humor, and are drawn with great knowledge and skill...."

It was Berryman's wishes when he gave his cartoons for permanent placement in the Library of Congress and the Corcoran Gallery, that future historians of our era would appreciate his work as an aid in illuminating the past historical events.

Clifford Berryman died peacefully at his home December 11, 1949.

No longer would the handsome artist's figure be one of Washington's familiar sights, known for his flowing windsor ties, gray in summer, black in winter, said to be a tribute to the Kentucky legislator, Senator Blackburn. It was he who first opened the doors of Washington for Berryman, and he who Berryman so admired as a young boy. It is thought perhaps some of the fine qualities for which Senator Blackburn was loved were bequeathed as a spiritual legacy to his protégé.

In honoring Clifford Berryman after he died, *The Washington Evening Star* shared its bereavement with its readers in his obituary published December 12, 1949:

"National leaders whom he gently lampooned and the public he served for more than half a century were saddened today by the death of Clifford K. Berryman, 80, editorial cartoonist of *The Evening Star.*

"The artist whose robust good humor had attracted thousands of followers down the years passed away peacefully at 11 a.m. yesterday at his home....

"One of the first to extend his sympathy to Mrs. Berryman was President Truman, who sent this telegram:

" 'A superb artist whose talent had been a national asset for more than half a century is lost to his far-flung public in the death of your devoted husband. He was a valued friend and I hasten to assure you that I share the sorrow which has been laid so heavily on you. To you and to all who mourn with you, I offer this assurance of heartfelt sympathy....'

"Mr. Berryman, whose vigor was a source of constant amazement to younger colleagues, had been ill since November 17. On that day he was reporting to his drawing board as usual when he collapsed at the entrance to The Star Building....

"A member of many Washington organizations, Mr. Berryman's first love was the Gridiron Club, of which he was the dean of active members. Since before he became a member, he had illustrated the menus.

"When the club held its annual mid-winter dinner Saturday, it was the first in 53 years that Mr. Berryman had missed. Realizing at the outset of his illness that he might not be able to attend, Mr. Berryman had requested that one of his guests, Crosby S. Noyes, a reporter for *The Star* be seated in his place.

"He recalled that Mr. Noyes' great-grandfather, the late Crosby S. Noyes, had taken him to his first dinner in 1896. Mr. Noyes was editor of *The Star*.

"With last Saturday's dinner on his mind. Mr. Berryman told his doctor he was surely going to remain alive during the day. He did not wish to sadden the ceremonies in which his son, James, at the annual meeting of the club, earlier in the day, would be elected vice president.

"The physician suggested that Mr. Berryman's willpower kept him alive Saturday night, and that he died peacefully in his sleep yesterday morning....

"His period included the Battle of Manila Bay, the discovery of the North Pole, the Kitty Hawk flight, the slayings at Sarajevo, the sinking of the Lusitania, the Lindbergh flight and Pearl Harbor.

"But Mr. Berryman's visual reporting stuck pretty well to the Washington scene, the Ballinger-Pinchot flight, the Wright flights at Fort Myer, the 1916 resistance of the little body of willful men in the Senate to the arming of merchant ships, the League of Nations fight, Teapot Dome, the court-packing fight and the battle over labor legislation under the New Deal and the Fair Deal....

"In the Berryman cartoons some had heroic roles, some played the villain: but none was exposed as a clown or a fool. Mr. Berryman pointed up the frailties of the parts they played without trespassing on the privacy of their own lives or personalities.

"There were thousands of others who never appeared in the Berryman cartoons who knew Mr. Berryman and counted him their friend —the many people who had heard his chalk talks, the fellow members of his church, the countless art students he had encouraged, former caddies at the Chevy Chase Club, the

Illustration 29. "Carrying Ballast." Original. *In the Collection of the Corcoran Gallery of Art, gift of the artist.*

Illustration 30. "Twas' the Afternoon of Christmas!" December 25, 1933. *Courtesy Library of Congress.*

27

Illustration 31. "Two Thanksgiving Days," November 23, 1939. Original. *In the Collection of the Corcoran Gallery of Art, gift of the artist.*

Illustration 32. After President Roosevelt's famous hunting expedition Berryman drew many humorous cartoons depicting real bears. Circa 1905. *Courtesy Theodore Roosevelt Collection, Harvard College Library.*

generations of copy boys who had taken his drawings to the engraver, the newsstand operator in The Star Building, who assisted him when he had the heart attack that sent him to the hospital.

"He was one of the most handsome as well as one of the most lovable men of 20th century Washington. His head was large and well shaped, his cheek was pink, his hair pure white and his broad face clean cut in profile. He wore the flowing tie that used to be the mark of the artist....He was a big man, six feet tall, with broad shoulders. Until the heart attack that sent him to the hospital, he always moved quickly and vigorously....

"He brought a gentility from his native Kentucky, the product of several generations of the best American culture. Good manners was part of his heritage, and his was a natural dignity that protected him from the backslapping of the vulgar.

"He had an unquestioning faith. Eighty years to Clifford Berryman were but an introduction to an unending life. He was a Presbyterian, as regular in his church attendance as in his contributions to *The Star*. He became a member of the church in his teens and since that day, he once said, he had never taken the Lord's name in vain.

"He had unfailing good health, but he had illness in his family that would have tested any parent. His response to that was action — and prayer. He told intimates his response to any difficulties in his life and in his work was prayer — constant prayer....

"Mr. Berryman was employed by Crosby S. Noyes, the editor, then nearing the end of a career that had started as a reporter for the paper before the Civil War.

"Mr. Berryman said it was Crosby Noyes who taught him the value of the gentle approach in cartooning. Shortly after he began to draw for the paper, President Roosevelt was having a feud with his party, and *The Star* editorial page was taking him to task for it. Mr. Berryman decided he would get into the fight. He adapted George Cruickshank's famous illustration from Dickens' Oliver Twist of the ruffian Bill Sykes about to strike a dog with a stick. But it was not Bill Sykes in the Berryman drawing. It was T.R. wielding the famous big stick and the dog was labeled G.O.P.

"As Mr. Berryman recalled it, Mr. Noyes looked at the picture a long time. Then he said:

" 'Berryman, this is much the strongest thing you've done for us. It's wonderful... Wonderful, and don't you ever draw another picture like it as long as you are here. It isn't your style at all.'

"The White House was a great deal more informal in those days, and Mr. Berryman and T.R. had many intimate talks....

"Another story he liked was about Andrew Carnegie. He drew a cartoon about the multimillionaire steel maker, and Mr. Carnegie wrote asking for the original. Mr. Berryman sent it to him with his compliments. Sometime afterward,

Illustration 33. Uncle Sam and his trusty companion have a hard time withstanding the political rain. Original. *Courtesy Smithsonian Institution.*

Illustration 34. Berryman's Bear introduces the "The Arts Club's guests of Honor," March 1, 1945. Original. *In the Collection of the Corcoran Gallery of Art, gift of the artist.*

Illustration 35. Clifford K. Berryman, called the Dean of the Nation's cartoonists, seated at his drafting board at *The Evening Star.* For more than 30 years from the date of his first cartoon on January 31, 1907, he drew a cartoon every day, seven days a week. This is believed to be a record among American cartoonists. *Reprinted by permission of the D.C. Public Library.*

when Mr. Carnegie was in Washington, he asked about the cartoonist.

" 'Is he quite normal?' the famed Scot wanted to know. 'I asked him for one of his drawings, and I got it with his compliments. That's the first time I ever got something for nothing.'..."

Numerous other tributes to the beloved artist were written in various newspapers and magazines.

In Reverend Frederick Brown Harris' tribute in *The Washington Evening Star* he wrote:

"There seems a certain appropriateness that his journey of fourscore years should end as Christmas chimes were pealing. He was in so many ways the embodiment of the Christmas spirit. Its zest, its glee, its merriment, its good will, its thought for others, with him was not a December specialty. He lived in that atmosphere and exuded that spirit the year around."

The day after Clifford Berryman died, cartoonist Herblock drew the famous little bear sadly sitting by the artist's empty chair with his paws covering his eyes in grief. *(Illustration 41).*

In an interview before the beloved artist died, he made this wonderful statement: "I'd rather draw cartoons than do anything else. Even if I had to work at some other job, I'd draw cartoons and give them away if necessary."

The memory of Clifford Berryman will live on through his drawings, but most of all he will long be remembered by his creation of the little bear, the likeness of which will live on forever in thousands of toy reproductions.

Illustration 36. On Clifford Berryman's 75th birthday, a group of senators honored him at a luncheon at the Capitol. Vice President Barkley (then Senator, left) and Senator Byrd of Virginia watched as Berryman blew out the candle on his birthday cake. *Courtesy Smithsonian Institution.*

Illustration 37. Clifford Berryman draws a cartoon commemorating the day, 50 years ago, when his first cartoon was published by *The Washington Post.* Berryman made the drawing when he visited *The Post* and called it "Back at the Post." *The Washington Post,* June 20, 1941. *Courtesy Library of Congress.*

Illustration 38. "How To Roll Your Own." The poor bear appears hot and frustrated as he desperately tries to learn how to roll a cigarette during the cigarette shortage in 1944. Original. *Courtesy Dr. and Mrs. Allen Mathies.*

Illustration 39. "Discovery of the North Pole by Admiral Peary." Original. *Courtesy Judith Waddell.*

A Chronology of Clifford K. Berryman

1869 - April 2nd, born in Woodford County, near Versailles, Kentucky. Son and tenth child of James T. and Sally C. Berryman. Father a planter and merchant.

1882 - Played hooky from school to hear Joseph C. S. Blackburn (then Representative, later Senator from Kentucky) deliver a campaign speech.

1886 - Graduated from Professor Henry's School for Boys, Versailles, Kentucky.
   - August 4, arrived in Washington, D.C.
   - Draftsman at U.S. Patent Office, Washington, D.C.

1893 - July 5th, married Kate G. Durfee of Washington, D.C.

1896 - Began work as cartoonist at *The Washington Post*
   - Attended first annual Gridiron Dinner as guest of Crosby S. Noyes, editor of *The Washington Star*.

1902 - November, creation of the "Teddy Bear" as a symbol for President Theodore Roosevelt.

1903 - Published Berryman's Cartoons of the 58th House: A Collection of Original Sketches of the Complete Membership, Washington, D.C.

1907 - January 31st, left *The Washington Post* to begin four decades as cartoonist at *The Washington Star*.

1916 - April 10th to May 4th, exhibition of drawings at the Corcoran Gallery of Art.

1921 - February 22nd, awarded honorary degree — Master of Arts - by George Washington University.

1924 - June 16th to October 29th, exhibition of drawings at the Corcoran Gallery of Art.

1926 - Elected President of the Gridiron Club.

1935 - Began sharing the cartoon space with his son, James Berryman, and Gib Crockett. Did three per week.

1943 - July 5th, exhibition of drawings at the Corcoran Gallery of Art; 50th wedding anniversary.

1944 - Awarded Pulitzer Prize for cartoon of August 29th, 1943, on manpower mobilization entitled "But where is the boat going?" with F.D.R. at the helm of a rowboat.

1945 - Exhibition of works at Library of Congress, including 1165 drawings published between 1896 and 1945.
   - Exhibition of works at the Corcoran Gallery of Art.

1948 - Received Distinguished Service Award from the Cosmopolitan Club.
   - April, exhibition of 33 drawings at Public Library devoted to District interest or affairs.

1949 - Exhibition of 105 cartoons at Public Library.
   - December 11th, died at home, Washington D.C.
   - Memorial exhibition of drawings at the Corcoran Gallery of Art.

Chronology courtesy of the Corcoran Chronicle, 1984.

Illustration 40. "A Tribute to Clifford Berryman" by Charles H. (Bill) Sykes of the *Evening Public Ledger* of Philadelphia, published in *The Evening Star* with Berryman's obituary on December 12, 1949. *Courtesy Smithsonian Institution.*

Illustration 41. The day after Clifford Berryman died (December 11, 1949) cartoonist Herblock drew this cartoon in *The Washington Post*. It shows the little Teddy Bear seated at the base of Berryman's empty chair covering his eyes in grief. *Courtesy Hobby House Press, Inc.* (From the Summer 1985 issue of *Teddy Bear and friends*®.)

Chapter Two

The Mystery Of The Two Berryman Cartoons "Drawing The Line In Mississippi"

During the past 12 years I have collected Teddy Bears and have been interested in their history. I have both read about and heard people tell the legendary story of President Theodore Roosevelt's 1902 Mississippi bear hunt, when he refused to shoot a captured "bear cub," and how Clifford K. Berryman, a well-known political cartoonist with *The Washington Post*, illustrated this sportsmanlike event in his famous cartoon "Drawing the Line in Mississippi."

When I began the research for this book on Clifford K. Berryman I discovered he drew two versions of this historical event.

During a visit to the Library of Congress in Washington, D.C., I methodically searched through the microfilm and found the first *Washington Post* cartoon Berryman drew of Roosevelt's hunt on November 16, 1902 (*Illustration 42*). This cartoon depicted a "large," realistic-looking bear, who appeared to tug hard on the long, heavy rope which was held tightly by his captor. Roosevelt was also portrayed "trim and serious" looking, with hand upraised refusing to shoot the helpless bruin.

The famous cartoon published thousands of times (*Illustration 43*) was not, it appears, the original drawing of the incident.

It appears, shortly after the first cartoon was published in *The Washington Post* on November 16, 1902, the Washington National Press Club requested the "original" of the Clifford K. Berryman drawing that

aroused such national attention. When it became apparent the original was missing, Berryman drew another version soon afterwards.

He chose to take a more whimsical approach with his second drawing (*Illustration 43*). The bear was now cartooned as an appealing "little cub" looking very scared. Its captor now appeared much larger in comparison and held the worried bruin securely by a short, right rope. Roosevelt, with the same hand in upraised position as the first cartoon, is drawn this time time as a more robust figure, his facial expression kind and forgiving.

For years this cartoon was one of the notable items in the National Press Club's collection of originals. In 1940, yet another mysterious disappearance occurred. During the redecoration of the club's headquarters this original second version of Berryman's cartoon "Drawing the Line in Mississippi" appeared missing!

To attempt to uncover the mystery of the two versions of the famous cartoon that surround the Teddy Bear's beginning, and the different accounts of the historical hunt, I researched further.

(These facts, I later learned, were reported by Peggy and Alan Bialosky in their 1980 edition of *The Teddy Bear Catalog*, Workman Publishing, New York, NY.)

Illustration 42. Clifford K. Berryman's first version of the famous cartoon, "Drawing the Line in Mississippi," as it appeared in the *Washington Post*, November 16, 1902. Note the **trim**, serious looking Roosevelt and the **large** captured bear, who appeared to tug hard on the long, heavy rope which was held tightly by his captor. *Courtesy Smithsonian Institution.*

DRAWING
THE LINE
IN MISSISSIPPI

Illustration 43. The second and most publicized version of Clifford K. Berryman's famous cartoon, "Drawing the Line in Mississippi," is somewhat changed from the original. Roosevelt is drawn with the same hand in upraised position, but this time he appears as a more robust figure, his facial expression kind and forgiving. The captured bear now resembles an appealing little **cub.** *Courtesy Smithsonian Institution.*

Chapter Three

The Real Story Of Theodore Roosevelt's 1902 Mississippi Bear Hunt

The controversy over the legendary story of Theodore Roosevelt's 1902 Mississippi bear hunt encompasses the different reports as to the size of the bear the fair-minded President refused to shoot.

The most famous report is that the bear was a defenseless little cub, but others state it was a tired older bear.

Inspired by the desire to learn the real story, I enthusiastically continued my research at the Library of Congress in Washington, D.C. I was overjoyed to be able to read the actual account of the historical event. My only regret is the information I discovered did not enhance the original legend we have all grown to know and love so well.

The following are highlights of President Theodore Roosevelt's famous 1902 bear hunt, as it was originally written in *The Washington Post*. (Similar information also appeared in *The Washington Evening Star* and *The New York Times*.)

November 12, 1902

TRIP OF PRESIDENT

Traveled Across Blue Grass State During Night.

Cincinnati, (Nov. 12) — "President Roosevelt is speeding down through Kentucky tonight on his way to Smedes, Miss., about twenty five miles north of Vicksburg, for a four days' bear hunt....

"The President however does not anticipate the pleasure of killing a bear so much as the pleasure of a few days complete recreation in the woods....

"To one who has hunted grizzlies in the Rockies black bear are not very big game. But hunting bear with horse and hounds will be a new experience for him...."

November 13, 1902

IN HAUNT OF BRUIN

President's Party Has Reached the Hunting Camp.

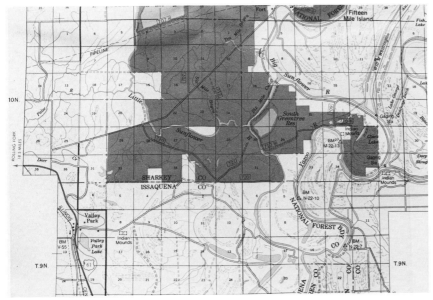

Illustration 44. The map shows the approximate location of President Roosevelt's famous Mississippi bear hunt. According to local guides the President, with his hunting party, crossed Deer Creek on horseback and camped on the west side of the Little Sunflower River. The actual event of Roosevelt's refusal to shoot the captured bear is presumed to have taken place at a water hole located on the east side of the Little Sunflower River. *Courtesy U.S.D.A. Forest Service.*

CLARKSDALE, Miss. (Nov. 13) — "President Roosevelt was joined at Memphis by members of the hunting party. President Stuyvesant Fish, of the Illinois Central; General Counsel Dickinson of the same road; John M. Parker, of New Orleans; John McElhenny [sic], formerly lieutenant of the Rough Riders; Maj. G. N. Helm, W. W. Mangum, and H. L. Foote. The latter three are big Mississippi planters and well-known bear hunters in this country. Mr. Foote is considered one of the best shots in the State.

"Mr. Parker has had charge of the preparation for the hunt, and the President appears to be greatly pleased with the arrangements. The camp is located fifteen miles east of Smedes, on the banks of the Little Sunflower River in a practically unbroken wilderness. There are no settlers for miles in any direction. The oak, ash and cypress forest is choked with an undergrowth of bud vine and thick, Mr. Parker said, as the hair on a dog's back. A trail has been cut to the camp, and horses have been provided for the members of the party.

"The camp itself consists of three sleeping tents and one cooking tent. Holt Collier, a negro who was a scout in the Confederate Army during the Civil War, and, who afterwards acted as a guide for Gen. Wade Hampton, has charge of the pack of hounds, which has been at the camp for a week. Among them is the most celebrated bear dog in the country. He is the property of Mr. Foote. This is his last hunt Mr. Parker told the President, as he is old and decrepit, though he had one more hunt in him, and when he opens his mouth it means bear.

"Collier, Mr. Parker said, was credited with having been in at the death of 1,000 bears. He is said to have killed nearly 150 in a single season.

" 'It will be rough work,' said Mr. Parker.

" 'That is exactly what I want,' replied President Roosevelt.

" 'But we will have bear meat for Sunday dinner' added Mr. Parker.

" 'Let us get the bear before we arrange for the dinner,' responded the President, laughing heartily...."

SMEDES, Miss. (Nov. 13) — "President Roosevelt and his party arrived here shortly before 4 o'clock this afternoon, and in their hunting costumes started soon afterwards for the camp on the Little Sunflower River. As the distance is about fifteen miles and the trail is rough and bad, the chances are that it was after dark before they reached the camp.

"Smedes is a siding on the Yazoo and Mississippi Valley Railway where cotton is loaded from the big Smedes plantations. A plantation store and residence of one of the

Illustration 45. President Theodore Roosevelt stands with several of the members of the hunting party that accompanied him on his 1902 historical Mississippi bear hunt. *Courtesy Theodore Roosevelt Collection, Harvard College Library.*

Illustration 46. President Roosevelt riding his horse by the Little Sunflower River during the famous bear hunt. *Courtesy Theodore Roosevelt Collection, Harvard College Library.*

Illustration 47. The remains of the Smedes plantation lodging place where Theodore Roosevelt visited during his bear hunting expedition in 1902. Unfortunately, this wonderful historical structure was demolished in 1983. *Information and photograph courtesy Southern States Images.*

managers are the only structures except negro cabins in sight.

"Work on the neighboring plantations was suspended this afternoon and several hundred negroes were at the siding when the train stopped.

"Most of the men sat on cotton bales...as the President stepped from the train.

"He was clad in hunting costume — riding trousers, heavy leather leggins, blue flannel shirt, corduroy coat and wore a brown slouch hat. Around his waist was buckled his cartridge belt and at his side hung his ivory-handled hunting knife. The other members of the party also wore hunting suits. While the guns, blankets and other small baggage were being loaded into a four-mule wagon...

November 14, 1902

ONE BEAR BAGGED

But It Did Not Fall a Trophy to President's Winchester.

SMEDES, Miss. (Nov. 14) — "A lean black bear which weighs 235 pounds is hanging up at the President's camp on the Little Sunflower, but to the regret of the entire party the first trophy of the hunt did not fall to the President's Winchester.

"The bear's trail was struck by the hounds soon after the party started this morning. The members of the party, except the President, Mr. Foote, Mr. Parker, and Holt Collier, had been stationed at the various crossings, and as soon as the dogs gave tongue, the President and his guides plunged through the dense underbrush in pursuit. Within a few minutes the dogs showed the direction the quarry was taking, and Holt Collier, with the instinct of an old bear hunter, immediately made up his mind where the animal would come out. To save the President needless hard riding through the brush, he directed Mr. Foote to take the President along the trail of a certain cut-off. This was done and the President and Mr. Foote rode to the assigned station.

"While on their way several swamp deer were jumped up but no effort was made to get a

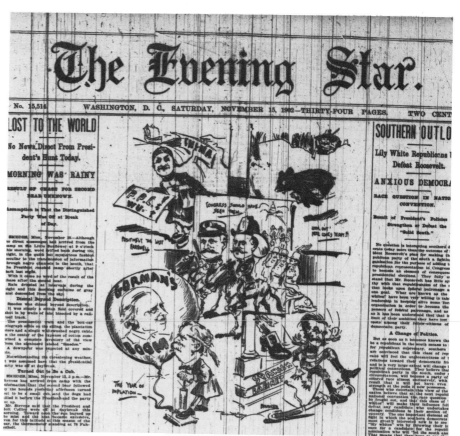

Illustration 48. *The Evening Star* cartoonist drew his version of Teddy Roosevelt's 1902 bear hunt in "Look Out! Here Comes Teddy," published on November 15, 1902. *Courtesy Library of Congress.*

shot at them. Then for several hours the President and Mr. Foote waited. The trail of the bear carried the yelping hounds out of hearing and shortly after noon Mr. Foote abandoned hope that the quarry would come back their way, and he and the President returned to camp for lunch. Had he remained, the President would have had a shot, as the bear with the pack at his heels crossed at almost the exact spot which Holt had indicated.

"About a mile beyond this point the Bruin, exhausted by its long race, ran into a water hole and turned upon the dogs....As the bear was making a sweep with its paw at another dog, Holt Collier jumped from his horse and, clutching his rifle, knocked the game over with a blow to the head. Then he blew his horn that the quarry had been brought to bay. A messenger was sent back for the President. Meantime Holt roped the bear and tied him to a tree. When the President arrived he would neither shoot it nor permit it to be shot.,

" 'Put it out of his misery' said he to Mr. Parker and the latter ended its life with his knife....

"The Associated Press correspondent arrived at the camp just as Holt Collier with his bear slung across the horse's haunches descended the river bank opposite.

" 'If the Colonel had stayed whar I put him' said the aggrieved Holt, 'he would'er done got this yere one.'....

"None of the small army of newspaper men and photographers who followed the President succeeded in reaching the camp today. The only newspaper men allowed there were the three press associations' representatives, who came with the party...."

November 15, 1902

BRUIN WAS IN LUCK

Mr. Roosevelt Again Failed to Get a Shot.

SMEDES, Miss. (Nov. 15) — "No fresh bear skin had been hung up today at the camp on the Little Sunflower up to 4:30 o'clock this afternoon. At this hour the President, Mr. McIlhenny, and Holt Collier were still in pursuit of a bear which was started early in the morning, but the remainder of the party had abandoned the chase, and twenty of the twenty-eight dogs had straggled back to camp, completed worn out.

"The President had hard luck today; twice he narrowly missed a chance for a shot. The pack

Illustration 49. An historical marker was unveiled at the Bear Hunt Reunion in Onward, Mississippi, to celebrate the 84th anniversary of President Theodore Roosevelt's 1902 famous bear hunt. From left to right are Sandra Desmonde, organizer of the event; Gordon Cotton, Director of the Vicksburg Court House Museum holding the Teddy Bear given to a young Vicksburg boy in 1907; Shelby Foote, grandson of Hugo Foote and Estelle Pearl, owner of the Onward Plantation.

split almost immediately after leaving this morning. Holt Collier with half the hounds, followed the trail of one bear down the river, and nothing had been heard of at 4 o'clock.

"The other bear went in the opposite direction, and gave the President, the other members of the party, and the rest of the dogs a merry chase. He was a big fellow, and kept well ahead of the dogs...."

November 16, 1902

QUIET DAY IN CAMP

President Had Bear Paws and 'Possum for Dinner.

SMEDES, Miss. (Nov. 16) — "Sunday was a quiet day at the President's camp on the Little Sunflower. There was no hunt, but the Presi-

dent and several members of the party spent a couple of hours in the morning rambling over the forest trails on their horses.

"Dinner was the chief event of the day. The menu included roast bear paws, 'possum, and sweet potatoes. Dinner was served in camp style on a rough pine board table set up in the open air. Tin plates and tin cups were used.

"There were not enough knives and forks to go around and the colored cook announced, to the amusement of everybody as the party sat down, that on account of the scarcity of the articles he had distributed them only to the 'Colonel' (as the President is invariably called in camp) and the 'foreign gentlemen.'

"The President is enjoying his outing very much. He has not had three days of such complete freedom and rest since he entered the White House.

"The insurgent newspaper men returned to the assault today. Having been repulsed on the landside by Mr. Mangum's pickets, they resolved today to try to effect an entry to the camp by the water route...."

Illustration 50. During my November 1986 visit to the first Bear Hunt Reunion in Mississippi, I could hardly contain my excitement when, with the help of a local guide, we saw the Little Sunflower River where, way back in 1902, Theodore Roosevelt had crossed during his famous bear hunt.

November 17, 1902

BEARS IN COMBINE

Conspiracy to Keep President from Shooting Them.

SMEDES, Miss. (Nov. 17) — "The bears in the swamp country around the President's camp on the Little Sunflower seemed to have effected a successful combination to prevent the President from having a single shot at one of them on the expedition.

"The only one the dogs started today fled in a northeasterly direction at the first cry of alarm and did not stop running until he reached the canebrakes about nine miles from camp. There he was overtaken by Mr. McDougal, one of the managers of the Smedes plantation, who

killed him at seventy paces. The President, who started this morning in the rain, with Holt Collier, did not hear the dogs after they first struck the trail.

"The President takes his ill-luck good-naturedly. He says it is simply the fortune of the chase, and that he will have a last try tomorrow. The bear killed today weighed 225 pounds...."

November 18, 1902

BEARS LEFT BEHIND

Bad Luck of the President Continued Without a Break.

"SMEDES, Miss. (Nov. 18) — "President Roosevelt's bear hunt in Mississippi is ended and he has not had even a shot at a bear. The last day of the chase was simply a repetition of the three preceding days, so far as his luck was concerned. Try as the hunters would, they could not get a bear within range of the President's rifle....

"Although the President had failed to kill a bear on this expedition, he has enjoyed his outing, and speaks in high praise of the hospitality that has been accorded him. He philosophically attributed his ill-fortune to the traditional hunters' luck, and says the next time he goes after bear he will arrange to stay long enough for the luck to change...."

For so long I had been familiar with the beautiful story of the cute "little bear cub" that the President refused to shoot that it was an emotional experience to realize the supposedly factual episode was only a fairy tale. It was like discovering there was no Santa Claus.

I hesitated to write the account of what actually happened on the hunt, but it is part of our history. Therefore, it is important we are aware of the real story.

Endeavoring to bring to light why there were different accounts of the legendary bear hunt, and two versions of the cartoon, I considered the two main characters involved: Theodore Roosevelt and Clifford Berryman.

Theodore Roosevelt is remembered for his love of nature and animals. (The Mississippi bear hunt incident shows this.) His passion for hunting bears in particular was not solely to kill them but to observe their natural habits.

Clifford Berryman knew the President well. He was also a kind, gentle man himself, who was loved and respected in Washington. He never drew a cartoon that offended his subject.

However, Berryman was not on the bear hunt (as some early accounts reported). The only newspaper men allowed were the three press association representatives who came with the party.

Is it possible Berryman felt the more whimsical approach should be taken when he drew the second version of his cartoon, "Drawing the Line in Mississippi." Can we surmise that by changing the original **large** older bear to a small, imploring **little cub**, it somehow also changed the story of the bear hunt to the fairy tale version that made the famous event a legend and far more appealing to the public.

Clifford Berryman passed away in 1949 and along with him his secret of the two cartoons, but what he left behind was far greater. By drawing his little Berryman Bear, which became his trademark, he inspired the creation in America of our favorite toy — the Teddy Bear.

On November 14, 1986, the first annual bear hunt reunion was held in Onward, Mississippi, in celebration of the 48th anniversary of the day President Roosevelt refused to shoot a bear.

When I read about this forthcoming event, I imagined how exciting it would be to visit this historical location and see the places I have been so intensely studying. So I made the necessary arrangements to attend.

At the reunion, I was thrilled to meet Shelby Foote of Memphis, Tennessee. He recalled the tales of his grandfather, Hugo Foote, who joined Roosevelt on the 1902 bear hunt.

One special guest stood out in the crowd: a wonderful elderly Teddy Bear that Roosevelt had given to a young Vicksburg boy in 1907 (*Illustration 156*).

An historical marker, dedicated to Teddy Roosevelt and his legendary hunt, was unveiled on U.S. 61 at the Onward store (*Illustration 49*). The impressive looking roadside plaque states that the famous hunt was held at Smedes, about two miles south of the store.

The event was organized by Sandra Desmonde of Greenville who approached Onward store owner Mae Wilson with her idea after reading about the 1902 bear hunt on the back of a menu at a Vicksburg restaurant.

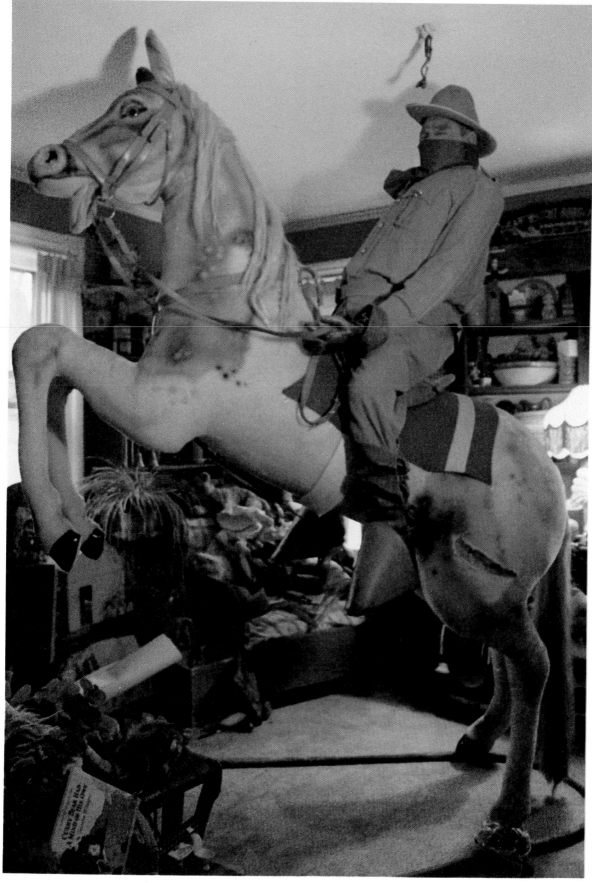

Color Illustration 1. 5ft 5in (153cm) tall life-size *Teddy Roosevelt on Horse*, manufactured by Steiff for Bloomingdale's Department Store in New York City. Roosevelt is dressed in his Rough Rider uniform and has a felt body, glass eyes and excelsior stuffing; his uniform is cotton and the hat is wool. The beige mohair horse is 8ft 2in (246cm) tall, 6ft (183cm) long with glass eyes, excelsior stuffing covering a metal frame, horsehair mane and leather reins, circa 1953. Extremely rare; only one known to exist in America. *Courtesy Ernie Eldridge and Anita Sebestyen. Photograph by Thomas E. Malloy.*

BACK HOME

"Well, once upon a time——"

Drawn by F. G. Cooper

Color Illustration 2. This colorful cartoon (not drawn by Berryman) is from a souvenir menu celebrating Theodore Roosevelt's return from his African Safari. It depicts Roosevelt relaxing among his huge trophies of his past hunting expeditions, with his friend the Teddy Bear affectionately seated on his lap listening to the President tell his "Once Upon A Time....." stories. *Courtesy Manhattan Sites, National Park Service.*

Color Illustration 3. Chromolithograph of President Roosevelt on a bear hunt. A very popular mass-produced series in its day. *Courtesy Manhattan Sites, National Park Service.*

Color Illustration 4. These magnificent examples of Teddy Bears were made by the German company Steiff, circa 1903. Early 1900 Steiff bears are undoubtedly some of the most collectible bears today. Their beautiful and distinguished characteristics, high quality of craftsmanship and unique features not only make them very desirable, but extremely difficult to locate.

Color Illustration 5. *Rough Rider Teddy* and his *Little Bear*, made by Teddy Bear artist Flore Emory. 18in (46cm) *Rough Rider* is of beige acrylic fur with natural brown eyes, hand-embroidered face and is fully jointed. His clothes are made from an old wool army blanket and he wears a felt hat, a wooden gun and metal glasses. 7in (18cm) *Little Bear* is of beige acrylic fur with black bead-type eyes, hand-embroidered face and is fully jointed. *Courtesy Flore Emory (Flore's Bears).*

Color Illustration 6. A 5ft (153cm) mannequin of Theodore Roosevelt and the 3ft (91cm) Teddy Bear (Flore Bear) tied to a tree depict the historical event in 1902 when Teddy Roosevelt refused to shoot a captured bear. This scene was created by myself and my husband, Wally. To help raise money for the abused children's home and to commemorate "1985" as the year of the Teddy Bear, we donated these items for a silent auction at one of my 1985 San Diego Teddy Bear events.

Color Illustration 7. Dentzel Carousel Tiger, circa 1910. Teddy Roosevelt is depicted charging up San Juan Hill in this unusual display of contemporary folklore. *From the collection of the Freels Foundation. Courtesy Tobin Fraley. Photograph by Gary Sinick. Copyright 1983.*

Color Illustration 8. Teddy Bears, a lithograph on a 24in (61cm) cloth. Political picture showing two bears returning from a successful hunt, carrying their game for the day. The bear on the left has "Washington D.C." written on his pouch. The bear on the right wears a Teddy Roosevelt style hat which states "I did it" on the brim. Copyright 1907, Schwab and Wolf, New York.

Color Illustration 9. In celebration of my new book on Clifford Berryman and Theodore Roosevelt, talented artist Beth Diane Hogan gave me a special one-of-a-kind gift. Inspired by one of Berryman's cartoons *(Illustration 79)*, Beth handcrafted this adorable little figurine of Teddy Roosevelt with his arm around Berryman's little bear. Made entirely of Fimo (a form of clay), this magnificent work of art is only 3in (8cm) tall.

Color Illustration 10. 8in (20cm) Steiff Teddy Bear, in original hunting outfit; of short white mohair with glass eyes, swivel head, excelsior stuffing and fully jointed, circa 1953. The accompanying Steiff booklet shows Roosevelt on a horse surrounded by bears in the same hunting attire. *Joan Sickler Collection.*

Color Illustration 11. 3¾in (10cm) china novelty toothpick holder shaped like a hollow tree stump with Teddy Roosevelt in military uniform kneeling, holding a "big stick" while a bear climbs the tree, circa 1907. Made in Germany.

Color Illustration 12. Early American Teddy Bear dressed in original Rough Rider outfit, representing Teddy Roosevelt. *Jan Gambil Collection.*

Color Illustration 13. Colorful picture of Teddy Roosevelt leading a procession of bears is in the center of this rare milk glass plate. *Beverly Port Collection.*

Color Illustration 14. In the Cracker Jack series of postcards, President Roosevelt is depicted chasing the Cracker Jack Bears up a tree. Copyright 1907, B. E. Mooreland, Rueckheim Bros., Eckstein, Chicago, U.S.A.

Color Illustration 15. Teddy Roosevelt's famous Bear Hunt influenced even the very young. In this postcard "One of Us Must Die," the little boy posing as the hunter, stalks his quarry — the Teddy Bear. Copyright 1908, Campbell Art Co., N.Y.

Color Illustration 16. The young bear hunter proudly wearing his rough rid hat and gaiters has fun with his Teddy Bear making believe he is the Preside coming home from a successful hunt. The caption "Delighted" also refers one of the President's famous expressions. Copyright 1907, Gutmann a Gutmann.

48

The Development of Clifford K. Berryman's Famous Cartoon Symbol — The Teddy Bear

Of all the 15,000 cartoons Clifford K. Berryman drew throughout his productive and eventful life, he gained the most recognition and fame from his cartoon "Drawing the Line in Mississippi" (for information on the cartoon, please refer to Chapter Two, "The Mystery of the Two Cartoons — 'Drawing the Line in Mississippi' ").

From this famous cartoon evolved Berryman's renowned, lovable little bear, better known to us as the Teddy Bear.

Berryman's bear first made his grand debut in the original cartoon, "Drawing the Line in Mississippi," published in *The Washington Post* on November 16, 1902 *(Illustration 51)*. Unlike his adorable diminutive Teddy Bear with whom we are familiar today, this drawing was of a "large," frightened, realistic-looking bear, whose life was spared by the kindhearted President during his legendary Mississippi bear hunt.

As *The Washington Post* continued its daily reports of Roosevelt's four-day Mississippi bear expedition, Berryman did not draw another cartoon regarding the hunt until November 19 *(Illustration 52)*. This cartoon, entitled "After a Twentieth Century Bear Hunt," portrayed a worried looking "little" bruin being dragged out of the canebrakes (tall, thick growth of cane) by a rope with a

tag attached "Back to the Zoo." Following close behind is the President, a tired hunting party, their exhausted hound dogs and a caravan. In this drawing the bear is smaller and whimsical, but still is depicted as a more realistic bear. It has not yet taken the shape to resemble a Teddy Bear.

In the month that followed the notorious hunt, we observe many changes in the shape and form of the bear Berryman drew for *The Washington Post*. In *Illustrations 53* and *54*, Berryman portrayed the bear (who has not yet taken the shape of the friendly little Teddy Bear) as being one that was spared by the President. It appears it was not until November 30, 1902, in Berryman's *Washington Post* cartoon "Ready For The Fray" *(Illustration 55)*, that he drew a bear with President Roosevelt at the White House. In the cartoon, the bear, appearing frightened by his new environment, has suddenly been transformed into the adorable little bruin with whom we are familiar. Note the development of his character already taking shape by the expression the clever cartoonist has given his face.

Thereafter, with each new cartoon the bear's personality and appearance grew more and more appealing.

Letters poured into *The Washington Post* praising Berryman's cartoons. The readers said they would like

Illustration 51. Clifford Berryman's bear first made his grand debut in his original cartoon "Drawing the Line in Mississippi," published in *The Washington Post* on November 16, 1902. Unlike his diminutive Teddy Bear, with whom we are familiar today, this drawing was a "large," frightened, realistic-looking bear, whose life was spared by the kindhearted president during his legendary Mississippi bear hunt. *Courtesy Library of Congress.*

Illustration 52. Succeeding Berryman's cartoon, "Drawing the Line in Mississippi" *(Illustration 51)* in *The Washington Post*, this cartoon, "After a Twentieth Century Bear Hunt," pictorially reported the end of Roosevelt's Mississippi bear hunt (November 19, 1902). Berryman portrayed a worried-looking "little" bruin being dragged out of the canebrakes by a rope with a tag attached "Back to the Zoo." Following close behind is the President, a tired hunting party, their exhausted hound dogs and a caravan. Note in this drawing the bear is "smaller" and whimsical but still is depicted as a more realistic bear. *Courtesy Library of Congress.*

Illustration 53. Following the cartoon "After a Twentieth Century Bear Hunt" *(Illustration 52)*, it appears Berryman did not draw another bear in *The Washington Post* until November 27, 1902. In the bottom right-hand corner of a montage entitled "They're So Thankful," a little bear is seated in a tree, arms folded, looking very relieved as he says he's so thankful "That He Didn't Land in the White House." Note how the bear has taken a definite change simulating a more human pose and facial expression. *Courtesy Library of Congress.*

to see more of this amusing little creature which had a magical way of making them laugh and feel happy. Admirers of the little bear anxiously awaited each new cartoon to witness his next mischievous and cunning antic.

Wellington Brink, a personal friend of Clifford Berryman, states in his article in *Good Old Days* magazine entitled "He Gave Us the Teddy Bear," the little bear made friends immediately. He went on to comment that the morning after it first appeared in the paper, William E. Chandler, the President of the Spanish Claims Commission and a former senator from New Hampshire, called the artist to tell him that he and Senator Henry Cabot Lodge laughed heartily at the little bear in the cartoon and hoped that Mr. Berryman would continue to draw him.

The public response was so overwhelming that the little cartoon character became his "dingbat" (cartoonist symbol) and an integral part of his drawings.

Soon novelty makers saw the opportunity to reproduce it as a toy. The "Teddy Bear" vogue swept the nation. Practically every major American city had at least one or two Teddy Bear factories. This lovable furry creature had captured the hearts of little people everywhere. Never before had anything compared to the craze of the Teddy Bear.

Clifford Berryman, however, never capitalized commercially on his creation of the bear, leaving it open for toy manufacturers. The artist could have made a million dollars, but instead he would tell people, "If it has given pleasure to children, that's reward enough for me."

He also commented that the thought of creating a bear toy never entered his head. The kind, generous man that he was just took pleasure in continuing to delight people with his creative drawings of the little bear.

Berryman referred to his new symbol as the "Roosevelt" bear and thereafter whenever he cartooned the President, the little bear was on hand.

Theodore Roosevelt, amused by the constant appearance of his new little companion, called the Berryman's cartoons "bully," even when he was the butt of them. The little bear was often shown in conversation with the President, to make the point of the cartoon.

Meeting Berryman later, the President said, "That little bear of yours has put the doll baby out of business."

Mark Sullivan in Volume 11 of *Our Times* gives credit to Mr. Berryman for the Teddy Bear saying:

"The Teddy Bear, beginning with Berryman's original cartoon, was repeated thousands of millions of times: in countless variations, pictorial and verbal, prose and verse; on the stage and in political debate; in satire or in humorous friendliness. Toy makers took advantage of its vogue; it became more common in the hands of children than the wooly lamb. For

Republican conventions and meetings associated with Roosevelt, the 'Teddy Bear' became the standard decoration, more in evidence than the eagle, and only less usual than the Stars and Stripes."

Because of his association with Teddy Roosevelt (for more information please refer to Chapter Five, "Theodore Roosevelt and the Teddy Bear"), Clifford Berryman would generally cartoon his bear when drawing the President. However, in Berryman's cartoons, together with the "dove of peace," the little bear also became a close friend of Uncle Sam.

A beautiful Berryman cartoon, "Nice Little Bird" *(Illustration 67)*, portrays these three characters representing, in their own way, love, peace and happiness.

The Berryman Bear became adored throughout the nation and the news ultimately spread aboard. Even other cartoonists adopted Berryman's Bear *(Illustration 68)*.

The generous, innovative artist drew numerous special cartoons for his friends. The bear often decorated

Illustration 54. Just two days after Berryman's cartoon, "They're So Thankful" *(Illustration 53)*, is when the talented artist drew the bear again. He drew this cartoon, "Consolation from Bruin." A small bear (not very cute) tells the lion "Don't worry: You may escape. I did." In this cartoon and *Illustration 53*, Berryman has portrayed the bear as being one that escaped President Roosevelt. *The Washington Post*, November 29, 1902. *Courtesy Library of Congress.*

READY FOR THE FRAY.

Illustration 55. The subsequent Berryman cartoon portraying a bear following "Consolation from Bruin" *(Illustration 54)*, was "Ready For The Fray," published in *The Washington Post* on November 30, 1902. It appears to be the first cartoon Berryman drew of the bear with President Theodore Roosevelt at the White House. Note how the bear, appearing frightened by his new environment, has suddenly become the adorable little bear with whom we are familiar, his character starting to develop by the expression the clever cartoonist has given to his face. *Courtesy Library of Congress.*

Illustration 56. "Christmas Dreams," *The Washington Post*, December 25, 1902. Berryman humorously cartooned his new little cartoon character having a horrifying dream of his "bear skin" decorating the White House for Christmas! *Courtesy Library of Congress.*

Illustration 57. This intriguing Berryman cartoon, "Columbia in Wonderland," appeared on page three of *The Washington Post*, December 25, 1902, the same day as *Illustration 56* appeared. *Courtesy Library of Congress.*

One day of Black and Tans grown tired,
  Likewise of Lily Whites,
Columbia to sleep retired
  And dreamed of startling sights.

And probably the funniest one,
  The most grotesque and queer,
Was that of men, each with a gun,
  Just as depicted here.

She saw two forms with Yankee pluck
  Go forth to do and dare,
And one was Teddy shooting duck—
  One, Grover shooting bear.

The ducks, all clad in fur, looked bored
  And could not slaughtered be;
The bears had wings and safely soared
  With quacks of ghoulish glee.

Too Much Up-to-dateness in This Mode of Hunting Bear to Suit the President.

Illustration 58. "Make Way for The President." "Too Much Up-to-dateness in This Mode of Hunting Bear to Suit the President," *The Washington Post*, February 1, 1903. *Courtesy Library of Congress.*

Illustration 59. "Misfit Valentines," *The Washington Post*, February 14, 1903. Featured in the center cartoon as part of a montage is an unnatural sight — bears coming out of the canebrakes "happily following" the feared great hunter, Teddy Roosevelt, the complete opposite version of *Illustration 58. Courtesy Library of Congress.*

Illustration 60. "Out of the Woods," *The Washington Post*, April 26, 1903. *Courtesy Library of Congress.*

Illustration 61. On the day of Theodore Roosevelt's inauguration, March 4, 1905, Berryman drew two cartoons on page one of *The Washington Post*, "The Evolution of The Roosevelt Bear" (Berryman's name for his cartoon symbol) and "The Original Roosevelt Man." The adorable Roosevelt bear cartoon beginning with the President's capture of the bear in 1902, depicts stages of his eventful life up until Roosevelt's inauguration day. *Courtesy Library of Congress.*

Illustration 62. "Roosevelt Bears Make A Christmas Visit," *The Washington Post*, December 26, 1906. Berryman always referred to his cartoon character as the "Roosevelt Bear." *Courtesy Library of Congress.*

Illustration 63. "Listen in Everybody!" Original. *Courtesy Judith Waddell.*

Illustration 64. "The New Uncle Sam." Original. *In the Collection of the Corcoran Gallery of Art, gift of the artist.*

his letters in some form or another. Invitations were answered either by gleeful little bear(s) caricatured writing words of acceptance or, in the case when Berryman was unable to accept the engagement, his trusty friend could be drawn in a frenzy, completely wrapped up in his other invitations *(Illustration 73)*, or crying while delivering his "regrets" *(Illustrations 74* and *75).*

Recipients of birthday, anniversary, wedding and Christmas greetings welcomed the familiar appearance of the friendly little character on Berryman's cards or letters *(Illustration 71)*. Each newborn child in the Berryman family was presented with a personal treasure, a very special greeting with the familiar bear *(Illustrations 69* and *70).*

In later years the popular little character made fewer appearances in the cartoons Berryman drew for the newspaper. However, the following letter from an admirer of Berryman's Teddy Bear, written to the editor of *The Washington Evening Star* in April 23, 1939, is just one example of the strong influence and everlasting love people developed for the irresistible little bruin:

"I trust I am not wrong in thinking that there are others than myself who are willing to make acknowledgement to a bit of sentiment for those things which have come through long association to be identified as a part of our everyday life in the old 'home town'. One of these, surely, is the daily cartoon of C. K. Berryman in *The Evening Star*, the initial appearance of which must certainly be shrouded in the mists of antiquity....

"Mr. Berryman's cartoons are now an institution. So much so that I feel that we, the people, have something of a vested right in them. In this view I hope I may be forgiven for remarking that it seems to me regrettable that of late years this master artist has more and more frequently failed to stamp his creations with that truly distinctive hallmark which we have learned to love so well — the little white-faced 'Teddy Bear.'

"Each evening I look for it, but, too often, in vain.

"There is ever a fascination in peering behind the scenes — whether they be those of the stage, the political arena or just a simple picture. Many great and moving cartoons have come from Mr. Berryman's pen. Some have stirred our mirth exceedingly; others have made us very sad. But always, when the little bear was there, we could see beyond the two-dimensional limitation of lines upon paper. We could be sure, if the little fellow were shown gleefully rolled on his back, that Mr. Berryman was not just grinding out a picturization by order of that stern and fearsome man, the editor, but was really putting his heart into it and enjoying as much as we, the amusing result of his drafts-

Illustration 65. "Looks Like the Real Thing There." Original. *Courtesy The Smithsonian Institution.*

manship. And if the diminutive bruin sat in the corner with downcast eyes, beside the darkly draped coffin, we knew that Mr. Berryman was personally saying to us, 'I, too, share in your sorrow.'

"If an apology is due for this harsh complaint, then it is freely tendered, but I shall still maintain that a lot of us miss that wee furry rascal when he is away."

President Roosevelt even expressed his disappointment when the familiar Teddy Bear was absent from the cartoon. In a letter he wrote to Berryman on January 9, 1912, he said, "I was immensely amused by the cartoon (though I minded the absence of the Teddy Bear...)."

The story of an amusing complication that arose some years after Berryman first created his little bear, was written in *The Washington Evening Star* on June 1943: Robert W. Satterfield cartoonist of the *Cleveland Leader* started to adopt the Teddy Bear for use in his own cartoons and sought to patent it.

One day in 1913 to his surprise, Mr. Berryman received a registered letter from Mr. Satterfield's attorney ordering him to stop drawing his bear as it would infringe upon the Cleveland cartoonist's impending patent. Because of his years in the Patent Office, Berryman knew that the drawing of a bear could not be

patented. He returned a receipt for the registered letter covered with executions of his original bear.

Somewhat later the Cleveland attorney came to Washington personally, and threatened Mr. Berryman with prosecution. Having received no satisfaction from the cartoonist, the lawyer said he wanted to see a high official of *The Washington Evening Star.*

"All right," the artist told him, "but close the door quietly when you go out of his office. He has an awful temper when he is annoyed."

That ended the threatened suit.

Clifford Berryman became known throughout the world as "The Teddy Bear Man." The kind, thoughtful philosopher's creation of the jovial little fellow that aroused the childish feeling of happiness and laughter in people became a representation of all that was good in the world. The bear symbolizes many of Berryman's own inestimable qualities.

A segment taken from a tribute to Cliff in *The Washington Evening Star* on his 70th birthday describes this eminent man's wonderful personality and his love of life:

"Could any man, reaching three score years and ten, ask for more than to know that he has taught us the value of a smile?

"Few men have squeezed from the long years the joy of life and living that Cliff has

57

known, not only for himself but for the thousands who look forward each day to their quiet chuckle with him in the evening. Living to Cliff, has been a joyous adventure, with another cartoon and another laugh always ahead. He approaches each day's task, and he has been doing it now for 50 years, with all the zest of a small boy heading for a picnic."

On March 27, 1949, just nine and one-half months before Berryman died, a newspaper story, entitled "Teddy Bear Creator Still on the Job at 80," tells of the historical cartoon that Berryman drew in 1902, and how the stern New Englander, Senator Henry Cabot Lodge, then urged the cartoonist to continue to draw his new cartoon character.

Berryman did, of course, continue and his precious little bear became an integral part of his eventful life. It was even present at the reading of his will. The typewritten document conveyed the same conventional surface impression as thousands of wills before, but the last of the four pages were different. There, beside the familiar slanting signature of its creator, peeked the little Teddy Bear.

Illustration 66. "The Older I Grow, The More I Love the Atlantic Ocean," August 18, 1939. Original. *In the Collection of the Corcoran Gallery of Art, gift of the artist.*

Illustration 67. "Nice Little Bird." In Berryman's cartoons, together with the dove of peace, the little bear also became a friend of Uncle Sam. This beautiful cartoon portrays these three characters, representing in their own way love, peace and happiness. Original. *In the Collection of the Corcoran Gallery of Art, gift of the artist.*

A SPECTER IN THE CANE BRAKE

Illustration 68. "Presidential Cane Brake" by Kirk Russell. Here we see another cartoonist has incorporated his own version of Berryman's popular bear when depicting President Roosevelt. *Courtesy The University of Hartford.*

Illustration 69. Each newborn child in the Berryman family was presented with a personal treasure, a very special greeting with the familiar bear. This adorable cartoon was for Berryman's grandniece, Lewise. Original. *Courtesy Dr. and Mrs. Allen Mathies.*

Illustration 70. Celebrating her birth, Betty Ruth (Clifford Berryman's grandniece) received a personalized cartoon from her Uncle Cliff. Original. *Courtesy Betty Ruth Austin.*

As we move into a new home and prepare to enjoy a Christmas of contentment, renewed faith and hope for the world's future, we wish for you the season's blessings and a New Year in which dreams of peace, freedom and progress will become realities.

Mr. & Mrs. C.K. Berryman
Miss Florence S. Berryman

1939.

BANCROFT PLACE
NORTHWEST.

THIS IS THE STREET—
THAT'S THE NUMBER

Illustration 71. The Berryman family Christmas cards were most welcomed by their recipients especially since they were illustrated by the famous cartoonist. Berryman would painstakingly tint scores of them by hand. His daughter Florence composed the verses. This particular Christmas card celebrated the move into their new house in 1939. *Courtesy Library of Congress.*

Illustration 72. Berryman's famous Teddy Bear often appeared beside his signature. Photograph of Clifford Berryman in 1913. *Courtesy Betty Ruth Austin.*

Illustration 73. Clifford Berryman's replies to invitations were often answered by drawings of his familiar bear. In the case of the busy cartoonist being unable to accept the engagement, his trusty friend could be drawn in a frenzy completely "wrapped up" in other invitations. November 14, 1932. *Courtesy Library of Congress.*

Illustration 74. Tearful little bears regretfully answer invitations the active Berryman is unable to accept. March 16, 1932. *Courtesy Library of Congress.*

Illustration 75. Although the recipients' are dismayed at receiving the busy cartoonist's regrets to their invitations, the drawings of Berryman's bear delivering the message is a treasured consolation. April 16, 1923. *Courtesy Library of Congress.*

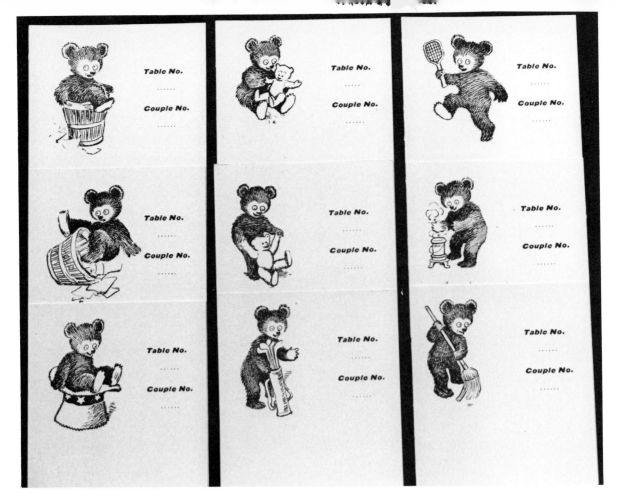

Illustration 76. Clifford Berryman even found time to illustrate place cards with numerous variations of his mischievous little bear for the Washington Heights Presbyterian Church, the church which the kind and gentle artist helped build and attended for 45 years.

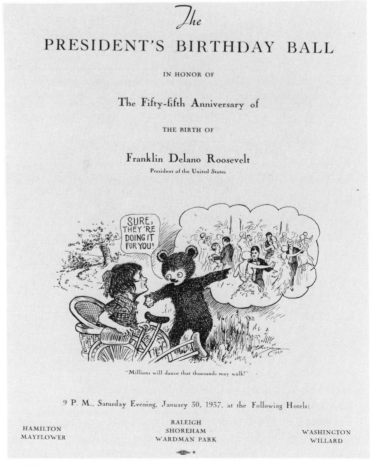

Illustration 77. This drawing the sensitive cartoonist drew for the program of the fund-raising ball, in honor of President Franklin D. Roosevelt's 55th birthday, would touch anyone's heart and inspire them to help the crippled children. January 30, 1937. *Courtesy Library of Congress.*

Illustration 78. Clifford Berryman's benevolent Teddy Bears are often found helping to raise funds for various charities. March 12, 1937. *Courtesy Library of Congress.*

Chapter Five

Theodore Roosevelt and the Teddy Bear

Illustration 79. Theodore Roosevelt in his Rough Rider uniform with his arm affectionately around Clifford Berryman's famous cartoon character — the Teddy Bear. *Courtesy Library of Congress.*

Even before that famous bear hunt, Theodore Roosevelt had been a familiar figure in Berryman's cartoons. The drawing of the legendary little bruin continued to appear, and become a popular addition to almost every Berryman Roosevelt-oriented cartoon.

However, it appears Roosevelt was originally embarrassed by the Mississippi incident. A letter to his friend, Philip Stewart (November 24, 1902), divulged that he felt his kind hosts (even with the best intentions) had turned the hunt into a cross between a hunt and a picnic. He had been unable to get a single shot at a bear. He also stated how the "comic press" had naturally jumped at the failure, and had done a good deal of laughing at the event!

When gifts of toy bears began arriving at the White House shortly afterwards, it appears the President soon saw the humorous side of the unlucky hunt. The following article from the *New York Herald* (December 28, 1902) was just the beginning of the association Roosevelt would have with bears in many different mediums in the years to come:

CHRISTMAS JOKERS SEND
TOY BEARS TO PRESIDENT
Mr. Roosevelt Enjoys the Humor of the Gifts
and Shows Them to Friends

"President Roosevelt had great success hunting bear at the White House Christmas morning. He started on the trail for the library, where the Christmas presents were assembled, and there he found three miniature bears waiting for him. They were of three varieties of the bruin tribe.

"One came from the sunny South, one from the Northwest and one from New York — a black, a brown and a grizzly. They were all addressed to the President, and he enjoyed the humor of the presentations equally as much as the members of his family.

"These toys in size and appearance were excellent imitations of the living animal. The one from the Northwest was a mechanical or dancing bear, and his performances created much merriment among the members of the household.

"The President displayed his dancing bear to friends who called at the White House Christmas Day."

On December 29, 1902, President Roosevelt wrote Clifford Berryman a letter expressing his delight with the little bear cartoons that had followed the original of the notorious hunt:

"My dear Mr. Berryman:

"I must thank you personally for the calendar. Mrs. Roosevelt and the children will be quite as amused with it as I am.

"We have all been delighted with the little bear cartoons. I begin to feel as if it was like those special signs of the early Egyptian Kings — I have forgotten their names — cartouches, is it not?

Illustration 80. Bears were not called Teddy Bears in *Playthings* magazine until this advertisement which appeared in their 1906 issue. Note they are referred to as "Teddy's Bears." *Courtesy Playthings.*

"I want very much to see you here in the near future and shall be glad if you will call some morning.

Sincerely yours,
Theodore Roosevelt."
(This letter is located in the Manuscript Department of the Library of Congress.)

Roosevelt began to refer to the little character with whom he was associated as the "Berryman Bear." On January 4, 1908, the President inscribed one of his photographs *(Illustration 92)* to the creator of his popular associate with the following notation:

"The creator of the 'Berryman Bear' always has the call on the Roosevelt administration! My dear Mr. Berryman, you have the real artist's ability to combine great cleverness and keen truthfulness with entire freedom from malice. Good citizens are your debtors. Ever your friend, Theodore Roosevelt."

Nevertheless, the Berryman Bear is known to us as the "Teddy Bear." How the bear received the name of "Teddy Bear" is yet another mystery. However, both of the most well-known tales give "Teddy" Roosevelt credit for the use of his name.

The famous American legend and family oral history comes from Benjamin Michtom *(Color Illustration 17)*, son of Russian immigrant Morris Michtom and his wife, Rose, who were inspired by Berryman's cartoons to create a little jointed bear.

Illustration 81. Cambridge University, June 1910. The students play a prank on President Roosevelt by placing a Teddy Bear in his path. *Courtesy Theodore Roosevelt Collection, Harvard College Library.*

Morris Michtom had always admired the President and wrote to him requesting his permission to christen the new toy bear cub "Teddy Bear" in memory of the incident. The busy President is said to have answered this letter on White House stationery in longhand, giving his okay, but, added he did not know how his name would ever help the stuffed animal business. (Unfortunately this letter has never been found to document this story.)

The Michtoms presented their newly-created bear to the Butler Brothers, a large wholesale company which is said, in 1903, to have bought the Michtom's entire stock of toy bears. Butler Brothers backed Michtom's credit with plush-producing mills and in a year mass production for the Ideal Novelty & Toy Company became a reality. The company shortened its name to the Ideal Toy Company in 1938. Benjamin presented an Ideal Bear (dated as a 1903 original [*Color

Illustration 18]) to President Theodore Roosevelt's grandson, Kermit, and his family (1963). The Roosevelts decided the Teddy Bear — named for the President — should be donated to the Smithsonian Institution.

According to a letter sent to Michtom from Mrs. Roosevelt, the bear almost did not make it: "I was about to get in touch with the Smithsonian about presenting them with the original bear when the children decided they didn't want to part with it yet."

Luckily, Mark and Anne Roosevelt, the President's great-grandchildren, changed their minds several months later (January 1964). The precious bear is now proudly on exhibit where he can be enjoyed and appreciated for many years to come.

Another well-known story is about Steiff bears at Alice Roosevelt's White House wedding in 1906. Guests were greeted by Steiff bears decorating the table. As a tribute to Teddy Roosevelt's legendary outdoorsman

THE TEDDY BEAR SAYS:

Mr. President, I feel blue,
And I scarce know what to do,
For I have been told to-day
That a third term you won't stay.
Tell me quickly its absurd,
This rumor that I just have heard,
For if to run you don't agree,
My finish I can plainly see.

THE LITTLE DOLLY SAYS

Dear Mr. President be firm,
And don't accept a third term,
Teddy Bears for years, you know
Have caused us dolls lots of woe,
Please don't run 'twill end this fad
And make every dolly glad.
We'll forgive the harm you've done
If you promise not to run.

A
THIRD
TERM
?

Providence Novelty Co.
Providence, R. I.

COPYRIGHT 1907,
BY T. R. GAINES, N. Y.

prowess, the stuffed animals were dressed as hunters and displayed among tents and fishermen surrounding goldfish bowls.

When the question was raised regarding the breed of the animals, a guest spoke up and said, "Why they're Teddy Bears of course."

Unfortunately, this amusing story has since been denied by people who attended the wedding. What does seem true, however, is that the Steiff Company was manufacturing Teddy Bears in 1903 (Illustration 101).

In Patricia N. Schoonmaker's book, A Collector's History of the Teddy Bear, she wrote this additional information which documents a period in which Steiff was making Teddy Bears:

"The trade magazine Playthings was established in 1903 and the first Teddy Bear advertisement appears in May, 1906;...

"The following account is taken from Playthings, 1906:

'Over in Germany there is a little old woman commanding a company of more than two thousand workers whose busy fingers fly from early morning till late at night cutting out, stitching up and putting together plush bears for the American market. The people here, grown-ups as well as children, have apparently gone crazy over these bears. Years and years ago this woman designed a pattern for a bear which was so natural and appealed so to youngsters that she was called the mother of the bears. Then she had a tiny shop in her house

Illustration 82. Two cute poems on this 1907 political postcard tell of the Teddy Bear's and doll's battle to be the most popular toy:

"THE TEDDY BEAR SAYS:
Mr. President, I feel blue,
And I scarce know what to do,
For I have been told to-day
That a third term you won't stay
Tell me quickly it's absurd,
This rumor that I just have heard,
For if to run you don't agree,
My finish I can plainly see."
"THE LITTLE DOLLY SAYS:
Dear Mr. President be firm,
And don't accept a third term,
Teddy Bears for years, you know,
Have caused us dolls lots of woe,
Please don't run 'twill end this fad
And make every dolly glad.
We'll forgive the harm you've done
If you promise not to run."
By T. R. Gaines, N.Y., Providence Novelty Co., published circa 1907. Bernard Greenhouse Collection.

Illustration 83. The dolls (most popular toy before the Teddy Bear) campaign against Theodore Roosevelt, hoping that with his defeat they will regain their popularity over the beloved Teddy Bear. Political postcard, circa 1907. *Bernard Greenhouse Collection.*

Illustration 84. Roosevelt Bear Toy. A tin Roosevelt jointed bear, 6¾in (17cm) long, rides a bike when string is threaded through the loop and the groove of the wheels. The hanging weight gives balance to the toy. Circa 1907.

and only a few young girls to help her. That was before the bear fad struck America. Now she has a factory that covers a whole square and the machinery and employees are worked week in and week out at high pressure because Young America must have his bears. As the orders pile in with every mail and cables arrive almost hourly the little old frau and her workers hold up their two thousand pairs of hands in consternation and wonder if every man, woman and child in America is searching for a whole family of bears.

'They are not far wrong. The entire country is in the clutches, or rather the embrace, of the plush bear. His Majesty Bruin now reigns.

'The bear rage started at the summer resorts along the Jersey shore, some say it was Atlantic City....

'Then other shops stocked up with them, and the big ones in New York found themselves overwhelmed with orders for Teddy Bears. By this time Young America had christened them, appropriately, too. Isn't the President the hero of every boy who longs to grow big enough to hold a gun to shoot bears and some day do just the very same things that 'Teddy' Roosevelt does? So Teddy the bears were named, and as Teddy they are known now the length and breadth of our country, as well as on the other side of the Atlantic....

'The mother of the bears, the little German frau, is almost at her wits' end to know what she is going to do. There is a fear that the supply of the brown and white plush will give out, and then what would she do, for they wouldn't be as good if they were made of any other color. One New York store, the largest we have, has already sold over sixty thousand Teddies, and every week it gets hundreds of dozens, which are bought up at once....."

An official publicity release from the Steiff firm (circa 1965) stated that it was not in fact the little German frau, Margarete, that created the Teddy Bear:

"In 1897, after completing his art studies in England and Germany, Margarete's nephew, Richard, joined the firm. While studying in Germany, he spent many hours sketching the playful brown bear cubs at Stuttgart's famous zoo. Working from these sketches, Richard designed a little toy bear, with moveable joints made of mohair plush (the first stuffed toy having moving joints). The first models were introduced in 1902 and found their way to America a year later, 1903."

Evidence of an occasion with President Roosevelt where "Steiff bears" were present, was recently discovered by my friend and Teddy Bear authority, Barbara Lauver. This event followed Theodore Roosevelt's return from his scientific expedition in Africa

Illustration 85. Rare cloth *Theodore Roosevelt* doll. *Courtesy Smithsonian Institution.*

(1910). The President gave a dinner in New York for the naturalists who accompanied him on his trip. (For information on Roosevelt's African expedition, please refer to Chapter Eight, "Theodore Roosevelt — 'The Man of His Youthful Dreams.' ") As a token of his appreciation, party favors of a Steiff Teddy Bear were set at each place setting. Attending this prestigious occasion was John Alden Loring, the youngest of the naturalists to accompany the President. Loring's Steiff

Illustration 86. Teddy and The Bear, Iron Mechanical Bank. On February 19, 1907, Charles A. Bailey of Cromwell, Connecticut, was granted patent number 844,910 for his invention and design of the Teddy and The Bear Bank. Final production was executed by the J. and E. Stevens Company of Cromwell, Connecticut. When a coin is inserted into the bank, the bear springs out of the tree stump. *Volpp Collection.*

Illustration 87. Schoenhut's "Teddy's Adventures in Africa," was based on Roosevelt's legendary African Safari. The toy company marketed the 53-piece, wooden jointed set of characters in 1909. The star of the collection is the remarkably designed Roosevelt doll wearing a khaki hunting outfit. Other finely carved members of the hunting expedition include appropriately attired natives, a photographer, a gun bearer and animals. *Courtesy Margaret Woodbury Strong Museum.*

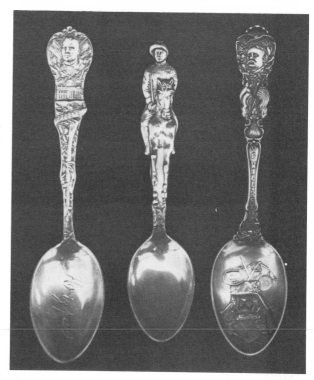

Illustration 88. Theodore Roosevelt Spoons. **Left:** Head of Roosevelt, White House, "Roosevelt," gun on handle; **back:** Rough Rider on horse, Roosevelt's home and hat; "Mizpah" engraved in bowl; markings read: "Watson-Newell Co. trademark sterling;" 6in (15cm). **Center:** Roosevelt on horseback; markings read: "Shepard Mfg. Co. trademark, sterling;" 5½in (13cm). **Right:** Head of Roosevelt, enameled flags, and "We Will Return" on handle; **back:** "1898 Libre Cuba," bowl engraved with various Rough Rider equipment (gun, hat, canteen, sword, backpack, gunbelt, stirrups); markings read: "Gorham, Mfg. Co. trademark, sterling, H10;" 6in (15cm). *Mimi Hiscox Collection.*

Illustration 89. Exhibit of Teddy Bear and Roosevelt memorabilia from the Lion's Room of the Theodore Roosevelt's Birthplace in New York City. *Courtesy Manhattan Sites, National Park Service.*

Illustration 90. Theodore Roosevelt memorabilia. **Top row, left to right:** iron bank, clay pipe. **Center, left to right:** stick pin, brass mechanical pin, stick pin. **Bottom row, left to right:** leather purse, glass change tray. *Courtesy Hakes Americana.*

Teddy Bear *(Color Illustration 21)* and this interesting story was brought to Barbara's attention at a toy show in March 1987, by a lady who had purchased the bear from Loring's heirs.

Roosevelt also became internationally associated with the Teddy Bear toy. Another humorous example happened during a visit to England *(Illustration 81)*. Roosevelt recalls the incident in a letter to his friend, David Gray (October 5, 1911):

"In Cambridge everything was more informal, and it was largely a reception by the students themselves. They greeted me just as the students of our own colleges would have greeted me. On my arrival they had formed in two long ranks, leaving a pathway for me to walk between them and at the final turn in this pathway they had a Teddy Bear seated on the pavement with outstretched paw to greet me; and when I was given my degree in the chapel the students had rigged a kind of pulley arrange-

ment by which they tried to let down a very large Teddy Bear upon me as I took the degree...."

Numerous jokes and pranks were played on the good-natured President about his association with the Teddy Bear. One popular joke of the period went: "If Theodore is President of the United States with his clothes on — What is he with his clothes off? — Teddy Bare!"

Because of Roosevelt's famous 1902 bear hunt and his relationship with the Teddy Bear, the popular President was often characterized in one form or another.

His eventful and adventuresome life was celebrated in numerous books, toys and games. His distinctive facial features and robust smile often adorned dishes, postcards, trays and song sheets. His name was used to advertise groceries, patriotism and self-improvement programs. He even became the subject of a 1907 Edison motion picture: *The Teddy Bears.* In an emotionally stirring version of *Goldilocks and the Three Bears*, Roosevelt is shown as the hero. Relating to the famous 1902 bear hunt, the hero rescues Goldilocks and then refuses to shoot the adorable baby bear.

Based on Roosevelt's legendary African safaris, the famous toy company, Schoenhut, marketed a 53-piece wooden jointed set of characters called "Teddie's Adventures in Africa" in 1909 *(Illustration 87).* The star of the collection is the remarkably designed Roosevelt doll. Wearing a khaki hunting outfit, the doll looks very much like its human inspiration. Other finely carved members of the hunting expedition include appropriately attired natives, a photographer, a gun bearer and various wild animals.

A notable series of bear related children's books were written in the early 1900s with the same family name as the President. *The Roosevelt Bears*, created by Paul Piper under the pen name of Seymor Eaton, were two huge bruins. Teddy B and Teddy G (Teddy B stands for black and Teddy G stands for gray — not bag and good as some people often think) looked more like real bears than Teddies, but their influence on the toy bear market was tremendous. Originally published serially in 20 leading daily newspapers, the notorious Roosevelt Bears' adventures were celebrated not only in books but on postcards, china, trays and buttons *(Color Illustrations 24, 25, 26 and 27).*

Despite Eaton's commercial success, many critics treated him with cold harshness, claiming he was an opportunist who sought financial gain by using the President's famous name. Eaton fought back with defensive press releases and even in the introduction to his books to justify his position he wrote: "Since the name 'Roosevelt' has been used in the story, it may be of public interest to know that President Roosevelt and his boys have been pleased with the story as it has appeared in serial form."

The publisher, George Haven Putnam, once said of the Teddy Bear: "Was there ever a greater compliment paid to the personality of a great political leader than in

Illustration 91. Teddy Roosevelt 1904 1¾in (5cm) diameter campaign button, manufactured by Torsch and Franz Badge Company of Baltimore, Maryland; extremely rare; only four specimens are known to exist. Taken from the Clifford Berryman cartoon, the button depicts Teddy and his running mate trailed by a Teddy Bear. This cartoon button was never made in large quantities or widely distributed as were so many T. R. button designs. It could have been a salesman's sample for which orders were never received, as was the case with many rare political buttons. In 1904, political campaign buttons were relatively new and manufacturers outdid themselves producing buttons of great beauty. It was possible this plain black and white button was overlooked amongst all the other colorful designs available. It appears this is the only known Roosevelt campaign button picturing the Teddy Bear. *Fred H. Jorgensen Collection.*

this association of his name with the pet cherished by children?"

There were hundreds of Teddy Roosevelt related items but the one that has proved the most popular of all time is the beloved Teddy Bear toy.

So associated did Roosevelt become with the Teddy Bear the Republicans adopted the popular bear as an important and delightful symbol for the President's election campaigns. Political postcards, trays, pins and momentos of all descriptions depicted Roosevelt with his friendly little companion.

However, in Patricia Schoonmaker's book, *A Collector's History of the Teddy Bear*, there was an interesting side to the Teddy Bear's relationship with Roosevelt's political campaign:

"Since the Teddy Bear became so closely associated with Theodore Roosevelt, those of the opposite political persuasion were reluctant to give Teddy Bears to their children at first. As

a result, Sears and Roebuck Company advertised in 1907 that Teddy Bears were not a fad or a campaign item, but something that had come to stay on merit alone."

Adorable, small-jointed Teddy Bears were known to have been distributed as a campaign giveaway on Roosevelt's cross-country tour during his second run for the presidency. It appears the bears were occasionally passed to the crowds from the campaign train at the various stops of his tour *(Color Illustration 20)*.

Teddy Roosevelt's great accomplishments as a man and United States President will always be remembered, but the special toy he lent his name to way back in 1902 will be with us forever. We honor Roosevelt for his part in the evolution of our undaunted little friend, the Teddy Bear, a toy that will continue to spread love, happiness and friendship throughout the country and the world.

Illustration 92. Theodore Roosevelt referred to Clifford Berryman's famous cartoon character with whom he was associated as the "Berryman Bear." On January 4, 1908, the president inscribed one of his photographs to the creator of his popular associate with the following notation: "The Creator of the 'Berryman Bear' always has the call on the Roosevelt administration! My dear Mr. Berryman, you have the real artist's ability to combine great cleverness and keen truthfulness with entire freedom from malice. Good citizens are your debtors. Ever your friend, Theodore Roosevelt." *Courtesy Florence Berryman.*

Illustration 93. Original Berryman cartoon and Roosevelt campaign buttons are exhibited at the Theodore Roosevelt Birthplace in New York City. *Courtesy Manhattan Sites, National Park Service.*

Illustration 94. Theodore Roosevelt tin novelty button, circa 1904, issued following Roosevelt's return from Africa. It bears a subliminal message in the tiger's teeth that reads, "Welcome, Teddy." *Richard Friz Collection.*

The public response was overwhelming after Berryman created his little cartoon character — the Teddy Bear. Soon novelty makers saw the opportunity to reproduce it as a toy. This lovable furry creature had captured the hearts of little people every where. The Teddy Bear vogue swept the nation and abroad.

Illustration 95. Early 1900s American Teddy Bears. Note the characteristics of long narrow bodies, fairly straight arms and legs, small feet and short bristle type mohair.

Illustration 96. The Ideal Novelty Company did not advertise Teddy Bears in *Playthings* magazine in 1906 and 1907. This advertisement was the only one in the 1908 issue by this famous American company. *Courtesy Playthings.*

Illustration 97. A Roosevelt Laughing Teddy Bear was advertised by the Columbia Teddy Manufacturers in 1907. "The Laughing Teddy Bear Laughs and Shows his Teeth at Tight Money, Hard Times and Pessimists" (referring to Teddy Roosevelt's philosophies). *Courtesy Playthings.*

Illustration 98. Margarete Steiff. Stricken by polio as a child and confined to a wheelchair, Margarete Steiff began to show her business acumen early in life. In 1889, the imaginative seamstress conceived the idea of sewing an elephant into a pincushion. Soon Margarete created a menagerie of felt animals. The children throughout southern Germany sang her praises. By the turn of the century Margarete's nephews (Paul, Richard, Hugo, Otto and Ernest) joined her and turned the soft felt toys into a big business. Margarete Steiff's motto was "only the best is good enough for our children." *Courtesy Steiff.*

Illustration 99. Richard Steiff (Margarete's nephew) entered the company in 1897. A graduate of art school, he was an important addition to the family team. While a student in Stuttgart, he spent many hours sketching at the Nills Animal Show. In 1902, after working with these drawings, he designed a young bear toy. *Courtesy Steiff.*

Illustration 100. Early 1900s Steiff Teddy Bears. Note the characteristics of elongated features, long nose, big feet, long arms (when sitting arms will extend over feet), especially large hump on back and metal "Steiff" button affixed to left ear (very often missing).

Neuheiten 1903-04.

Illustration 101. This original catalog page documents the fact that Steiff was making bears as early as 1903. Note the name Bar (Bear). The name Teddy was not yet being used. *Courtesy Steiff.*

Illustration 102. Group of early 1930s English Teddy Bears. Note the characteristics of large wide head, plump body, large ears, rexine paw pads (resembles painted oilcloth) and painted glass eyes.

Chapter Six

Other Early Cartoon-type Bears

"I find it good to regulate
    The organs of both small and great.
    It checks SICK HEADACHE, and the woe
    That sad DYSPEPTICS ever know.
    Besides, 'tis pleasant to the taste
    And none need gulp it down in haste.
    The sparkling liquid quickly charms

The Infant in the Mother's arms.
    While drooping age will strive to drain
    Each drop the goblet does contain.
    How seldom in our life we find
    A REMEDY and treat combined.
    This EFFERVESCENT SELTZER fine
    A blessing proves to me and mine."

Illustration 103. Amusing caricatures of bears were drawn by talented artist Palmer Cox to advertise Tarrant's Seltzer in 1887. *Patricia N. Schoonmaker Collection.*

Although real bears are one of the most powerful and feared of all animals in the world, they have been all-time favorites even prior to the creation and popularity of the Teddy Bear.

The late 1800s brought the magic of the circus. The famous western hunter and trapper Grizzly Adams (Illustration 104), introduced his own collection of wild animals, in 1860, to Phineas T. Barnum, creator of the Barnum and Bailey Circus. More than 20 ferocious grizzly bears were among the collection. Adams became a great favorite, displaying his courage by performing amazing feats, such as riding the back of the largest grizzly while leading two others by a heavy chain.

With their human actions and ability to walk erect on hind legs, bears were a natural to amuse and capture the attention of both the young and old. In Europe, Victorian children were familiar with dancing bears which performed in the streets.

This early fascination of bears inspired many artists to characterize bears in numerous variations.

Bears quickly became advertising spokesmen. Pettijohn's Breakfast Food was one example. Their motto was "Bear in Mind Our Trade Mark," with illustrations implying their cereal gave you the "strength of a bear."

In Patricia N. Schoonmaker's book, A Collector's History of the Teddy Bear, she writes of the famous artist Palmer Cox, creator of the well-known Brownies, who drew amusing caricatures of bears to advertise Tarrant Seltzer Aperient in 1887 (Illustration 103).

Behr upright pianos, which had won awards at the World's Industrial and Cotton Centennial Exposition in New Orleans, Louisiana, in 1888, used three spirited bruins to advertise their prestigious products (Illustration 105).

Another well-known artist, Richard Felton Outcault, gained his recognition for his Buster Brown and dog, Tige, which were published in many newspapers throughout the country (his son and daughter were models for Buster Brown and Mary Jane). Outcault drew a cartoon-type bear that apparently first appeared in a comic strip, "Pore Lil Moose" in the New York Herald, copyrighted in 1901 (Color Illustration 47). This bruin-type bear became popular around the period of Berryman's bear, in a series of valentine postcards, copyrighted in 1903 by Raphael Tuck in England.

In the postcard, the bear's appearance had slightly changed from the comic strip. The little bruin's muzzle now appeared light brown, somewhat resembling Berryman's white-faced Teddy Bear.

Beverly Port uncovered some interesting information on Outcault's bear in her column in the January/February 1987, issue of Teddy Bear and friends®: "On another signed Outcault valentine dated 1904 the little bear is called 'Billy'....(Color Illustration 48).

One of the most popular Teddy Bear comic strips in 1907 was "Little Johnny and the Teddy Bears." Published by Judge magazine, this all-color cartoon feature consisted of six illustrations with a story caption under each frame. They tell "uproarious adventures of six stuffed Teddy Bears who come to life by means of a wonderful elixir and with Johnny get into and out of all kinds of mischief" (Color Illustration 43).

With Clifford Berryman claiming nationwide popularity with his cartoon-type bear, other artists sought their opportunities and numerous versions of cartoon-type bears were created, but the magical appeal of Berryman's notorious bear could not be equaled.

Illustration 104. Famous western hunter and trapper Grizzly Adams, with his friend, "Ben Franklin." The big grizzly was just a few days old when Adams captured him. Adams' greyhound dog, Rambler, nursed the tiny cub along with her own newborn pups. As the bear grew up, a close bond developed between him and his master. *Artwork by Evelyn Gathings.*

Why do they wear those Medals?

Illustration 105. Bears were used as advertising spokesmen. These three high-spirited bears were used to advertise Behr upright pianos in 1888. *Patricia N. Schoonmaker Collection.*

Chapter Seven

Billy Possum
"Teddy's Unsuccessful Successor"

Another politically-derived symbol that proved not as successful when it attempted to infringe on the popularity of the Teddy Bear was the possum.

President Roosevelt's successor, William H. Taft, dined at a banquet in his honor held in Atlanta, Georgia. The then President-elect ordered "'possum and 'taters" as his main course. So taken was Taft with the possum delicacy he made the statement "For 'possum first, last and all the time."

The press capitalized on his speech and announced it was the death of the Teddy Bear (alluding to Theodore Roosevelt) and the beginning of a lifelong reign for possums (meaning William Taft).

Toy makers jumped at the opportunity to make the new stuffed animal mascot of the current political administration and "Billy Possum" was born (Illustration 119).

Even though the toy industry made every effort to artificially foist his merits on the public to create a popular successor to the Teddy Bear, poor Billy simply could not compete with Teddy.

Clifford Berryman did, however, cartoon Roosevelt's symbol of the Teddy Bear with the succeeding President, William Taft, in a number of political cartoons (Illustrations 125, 126, 127 and 128).

Just two days before Taft's inauguration and in commemoration of Roosevelt's retirement on March 4, 1909, Berryman's famous Teddy Bear was found on the steps of the Executive Mansion looking sad and bewildered as he pensively watched the belongings of his loyal companion (President Theodore Roosevelt) being loaded into a moving van. The sensitive cartoonist entitled the drawing "To Go Or Not To Go" (Illustration 124).

An amusing comment was made by Roosevelt to the newsmen about his successor, "Bill Taft is a fine fellow — but how you are going to miss me as a copy maker!"

According to an advertisement in The Evening Star, March 4, 1909, it was possums and not Teddy Bears that were the popular toy at Taft's inauguration. "'Billy Possums' are the 'hit' of the inauguration, and you should certainly take one home with you as a souvenir!...."

Teddy's rival was truly an astonishing little creature and was humorously drawn many times by Berryman, during various visits by the President to the south.

Whether it be the sport of hunting possum (Illustration 122) or foraging for a President's dinner as is the example in the cartoon, "Foraging for the Taft Dinner

Illustration 106. "Back in 'Possum land," The Evening Star, October 25, 1909. Courtesy Library of Congress.

FORAGING FOR THE TAFT DINNER IN GEORGIA.

Illustration 107. "Foraging For a Taft Dinner in Georgia," *The Evening Star*, January 13, 1909. William Taft was so impressed with a dinner of "'possum and 'taters" at an Atlanta, Georgia, banquet given in his honor, that he made the statement "For 'possum first, last and all the time". The press capitalized on this statement and thereafter associated Taft with the possum that soon became his new campaign symbol. *Courtesy Library of Congress.*

in Georgia" (Illustration 107), the talented cartoonist depicted the occasion amusingly and to the point, in the style in which he had established his prestigious reputation.

William Taft regarded Berryman as his close friend and inscribed on his likeness: "To the cartoonist who resisted always the common temptation to exaggerate a corporosity already too large and who made me better looking than I was."

Two interesting accounts from a January 1909 *Playthings* magazine first appeared in Patricia N. Schoonmaker's article, "Billie Possum, The Teddy Bear Rival," (*Teddy Bear and friends*®, fall 1983). They show the attempt the toy industry made to create a worthy successor to the Teddy Bear:

"The newest toy in the stuffed animal market is 'Billy 'Possum,' conceived by enterprising toymen immediately after President-elect William H. Taft ordered 'possum' and 'taters' as one of the dishes at the famous Atlanta banquet tendered to him by the patriotic citizens of Georgia. The idea in mind is to have 'Billy Possum' become the petted darling of the hour, a much loved playmate, the fad of the modish young woman of the day, and the mascot of the incoming political administration. Three sizes, life, medium and four inches long, of the little animal are being manufactured by one of the new 'possum' factories where several hundred hands are said to be at work on the wooly little animal, the texture of whose furry coat is exactly like that of his live or 'pretended-dead' brother of the woods.

"A well-known Georgia beauty and society woman claims to be the first to realize the possibilities for the sale of toy 'possum,' and in a recent interview she gave out some interesting data regarding the new stuffed animal.

" 'What was my inspiration? Why the incident of our good citizen, Mr. Asa Candler, hitting upon the humorous idea of having 'possum and 'taters, as one of the dishes at the Atlanta banquet.

" 'Why should not the 'possum, with his pleased countenance, be just as popular as the Teddy Bear. He is quite as mirth-giving as the little god Billiken,' for when you just mention the word 'possum it provokes a smile. With this thought I determined to do my part toward introducing the mascot of the coming administration to the little folks of the country, and certainly the 'possum is just as easy of imitation as the Teddy Bear.' "

The subsequent story in *Playthings* magazine attempted to keep the possum an appealing new toy to the buyers:

"From all sources come the praises of the quaint new stuffed animal toy, and one of them is so comprehensive and complete of Billy's likable qualities that we quote from it:

Postcards from an historian's point of view are valuable sources of information, clearly illustrating events of the past. The postcard illustrations within this chapter depict the political scene between Taft and Roosevelt and portray how the Teddy Bear and the possum became influential mascots.

Illustration 108. William Taft adopted the symbol of a possum to compete with Theodore Roosevelt's Teddy Bear. This rare 1909 political postcard by Crite shows Billy Possum about to devour the special meal for the day — "Roast Teddy Bear."

" 'No matter what the naturalists may say, there is little doubt that Billy 'Possum is at least a distant cousin of Teddy bear; but he has ever and ever so many traits that his relative does not possess. He has the same cozy, fuzzy hair, but there are dark understripes on Billy which are foreign to cousin Teddy. Bill's nose is much longer and more inquisitive looking, and he has a different kind of ear, and, best of all, he has a long, kinked, interesting tail by which he has learned to hang himself up in the most nonchalant manner. He'll swing from anything — a finger, a clothesline, a string, the edge of a table, the branch of a tree — on this wonderful tail, and balance himself like a gymnast while doing it. And, of course, when he wants to he can stand up and kick out at various angles, and squeak, and assume any number of absurd poses, with his funny kinked tail standing up perkily in back.

Illustration 109. "President Taft and his Mascot: 'Billy Possum,' " circa 1910, published by Frank J. Cohen & Son, Atlanta, Ga., U.S.A. *Mimi Hiscox Collection.*

Illustration 110. Uncle Sam is served the same dish, "Possum and Taters," with which President-elect William Taft made history during a banquet in Atlanta, Georgia. Copyright 1909 by Fred C. Lounsbury, blue series number 2517. *Mimi Hiscox Collection.*

" 'But the big surprise about Bill 'possum is not so much his tail, nor his pointed snout, nor his balancing powers, but the brand new form he has taken. In many, many cases Billy is as plump and solid as a little pig, but in the rest —well, he is an astonishing little creature.' "

However, no matter how many companies pushed the possum craze as "here to stay," the curious creature fell short of the magic of "the old reliable Teddy Bear." Information regarding the political battle between Theodore Roosevelt and William Taft is well represented on postcards depicting the historical events of that era.

Today, Billy Possum toys and related political memorabilia are extremely rare and desirable collectors' items.

Illustration 111. Political postcard showing Billie Possum passing the Teddy Bear on his way to the White House. At the bottom of the card are the words "Good Bye Teddy." Photographs of Theodore Roosevelt and William Taft can be seen in the corner of the card. This was one of a set. Copyright 1909, by Fred C. Lounsbury.

Illustration 112. Political postcard. Teddy is wishing Billie Possum (Taft's campaign spokesman) good luck after William Taft became President. Postmarked 1909, printed by Interstate Printing Co., Atlanta. *Courtesy Mimi Hiscox.*

Illustration 113. Even Uncle Sam is shown to be fascinated with the new possum toy, while the poor old Teddy Bear lies discarded on the floor. "Uncle Sam's New Toy." Copyright 1909 by Fred C. Lounsbury. Blue series #2517. *Courtesy Mimi Hiscox.*

Illustration 114. In this rare cartoon published in the *Atlanta Constitution*, Taft confidently confronts Roosevelt with his new campaign symbol, Billy Possum, while the defeated looking Teddy Bear looks on. *Courtesy Susan Brown Nicholson.*

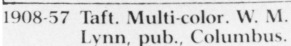

1908-57 Taft. Multi-color. W. M. Lynn, pub., Columbus.

Illustration 115. Political postcard. The Teddy Bear campaigns for William Taft, c. 1908, W. M. Lynn, pub, Columbus. *Courtesy Bernard L. Greenhouse.*

Illustration 116. Happy Billy Possum's Prosperity Puzzle is a most unusual campaign item, played by moving marbles up through a dimensional image of Taft's head and through the White House gate, while in one corner the Teddy Bear is seen packing his bags to leave. *Richard Friz Collection.*

Illustration 117. Even though the toy industry made every effort to artificially foist Billy Possum's merits on the public to create a popular successor to the Teddy Bear, poor Billie simply could not compete with Teddy. H. Fisher & Co. (New York City) manufactured the first version of the inquisitive Billy in 1909 as shown in this January advertisement. *Courtesy Playthings.*

Illustration 118. Toy makers jumped at the opportunity to make a new stuffed animal mascot of the current political administration and "Billy Possum" was born as shown in this February 1909 advertisement. *Courtesy Playthings.*

Illustration 119. By 1909 a number of manufacturers touted the praises of this "astonishing little creature." Billy Possum was a lifelike looking animal with a sense of humor who could (unlike his chubby relative) hang by this tail and assume a variety of positions, and was originally manufactured by H. Fisher & Co., (New York City) in 1909 with Strobel & Wilken company as distributors. Shortly afterwards Hahn & Amberg, the Novelty Animal House (New York City) promoted a 13in (33cm) possum made from the skin of a real opossum. Fortunately, most of the companies' smaller versions (as well as those of other toy makers, E. I. Horsman of New York City and Harman Manufacturing Company of New York City) predominantly used mohair plush cloth for Billy's coat. Even Steiff climbed on the bandwagon with a Billy Possum of their own, complete with the ever-present Steiff ear button.

Illustration 120. Billy Possum spoons and a fork. **Left:** embossed design of a possum hanging by his tail from an openwork branch of a tree with the words "Billy Possum" forming the handle, raised design of the White House in bowl with the word "Prosperity" above, markings read: "Mauser trademark, Sterling, patent April 1909," 6in (15cm). **Center:** embossed design of a possum climbing in the branches of a tree with the words "Billy Possum" on handle, markings read: "Wallace, Sterling, patent applied for," circa 1909, 5½in (13cm). **Right:** design of a possum hanging by his tail is on the handle with the words "Billie Possum," markings read: "Wallace, sterling, patent applied for," circa 1909, 5½in (13cm). *Mimi Hiscox Collection.*

Illustration 121. Left to right: aluminum bookmark of a Teddy Bear with the face of William Taft printed on the body; Billie Possum pin, 1908. *Courtesy Hakes Americana.*

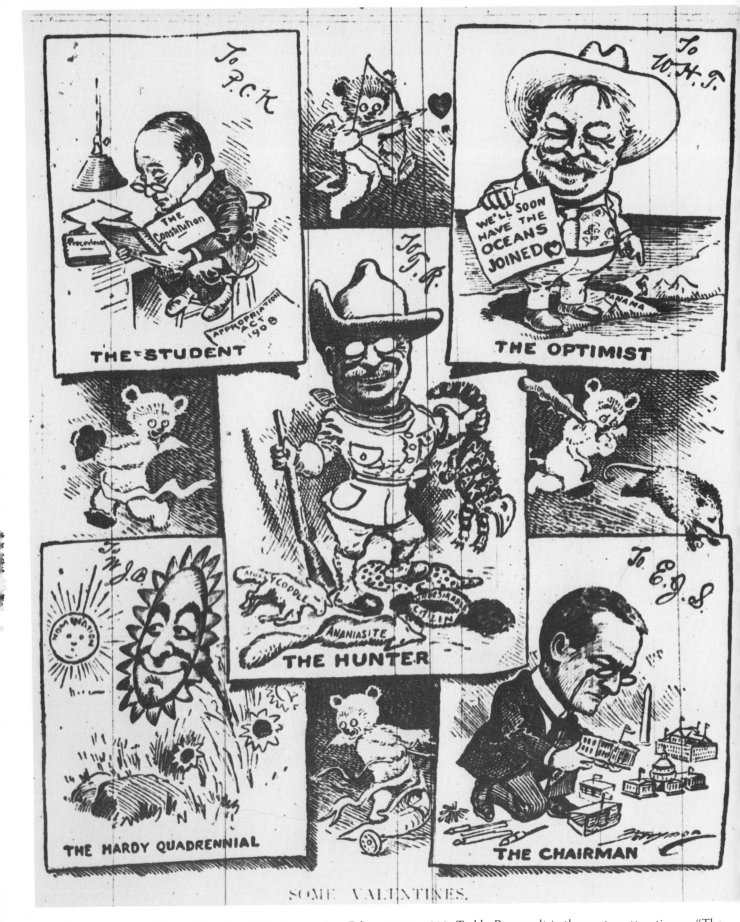

Illustration 122. "Some Valentines," *The Evening Star*, February 14, 1909. Teddy Roosevelt is the center attraction as "The Hunter." In with this eventful cartoon is the amusing drawing of the roguish little bear, chasing his rival the possum with his President's "big stick." *Courtesy Library of Congress.*

HIS INDEPENDENCE DAY.

MASTER BILLY TAFT. "THEY SAID I SHOULDN'T BE ABLE TO GET ALONG WITHOUT MY TEDDY BEAR—BUT I'LL SHOW 'EM!"

Illustration 123. Other cartoonists also associated Theodore Roosevelt with the popular Teddy Bear. In this cartoon jovial William Taft is depicted poking fun at Roosevelt dressed in a Teddy Bear suit. Published in *Punch* or *The London Charivari*, March 10, 1909.

Illustration 124. Just two days before Taft's inauguration and in commemoration of Roosevelt's retirement on March 4, 1909, Berryman's famous Teddy Bear was found on the steps of the Executive Mansion looking sad and bewildered as he pensively watched his Presidential companion's belongings loaded into a moving van. The sensitive cartoonist entitled the picture "To Go Or Not To Go," *The Evening Star*, March 2, 1909. *Courtesy Library of Congress.*

Illustration 125. Berryman's bear demonstrates his approval of the new President (Taft) by giving him a hug. *Courtesy Library of Congress.*

Illustration 126. The little bear puts down the "Welcome" mat with the jolly William Taft who had once been described as having "the most lovable personality...." *Courtesy of the Smithsonian Institution.*

Illustration 127. President Taft greets Diaz (President of Mexico) across the Mexican-United States border. Original. *Judith Waddell Collection.*

Illustration 128. "In the Political Agricultural Grounds," shows Taft as President. Original. *Judith Waddell Collection.*

ay of his dolls, past and present. The original Teddy bear is at upper left and some of his plastic toys are on the

Color Illustration 17. Benjamin Michtom, son of Morris Michtom, creator of the first known American Teddy Bear (Ideal Novelty Toy Company), stands in front of a case, displaying in the left-hand corner one of the early Ideal Teddy Bears. *Collier's Magazine*, December 17, 1949.

Color Illustration 18. Benjamin Michtom presented this Ideal Teddy Bear (dated as a 1903 original) to President Theodore Roosevelt's grandson, Kermit, and his family in 1963. The Roosevelts donated the Teddy Bear, named for the President, to the Smithsonian Institution in January 1964. *Courtesy Smithsonian Institution.*

Color Illustration 19. Ideal Teddy Bears, circa 1908. The famous American legend of Teddy's creation comes from the Ideal Toy Company, one of America's largest toy manufacturers and first known to make an American Teddy Bear. Note identifying characteristics of wide triangular head shape, low large ears and foot pad which comes to a point.

Color Illustration 20. It appears small Teddy Bears such as this were given away during President Roosevelt's cross-country whistle-stop campaign tour during his second run for the presidency. Note the resemblance to Clifford Berryman's cartoon bear, especially the eyes looking to one side. This 6in (15cm) bear was probably made by Ideal, is of honey colored mohair with a swivel neck, excelsior stuffing, jointed arms and legs and painted googly-type eyes; rare.

Color Illustration 21. This appealing old Steiff Teddy Bear was presented to John Alden Loring by President Theodore Roosevelt at a dinner in New York in 1909. The occasion was in honor of the naturalist that accompanied the President on his scientific expedition in Africa (1909). As a token of his appreciation, a gift of a Steiff Teddy Bear was set at each place setting. John Alden Loring was the youngest of the naturalists to accompany the President.

Color Illustration 22. Evidence of the influence of Seymour Eaton's Roosevelt Bears can be found on Teddy Bear clothes. The names of Teddy B. and Teddy G. were embroidered on suits and knitted sweaters.

Color Illustration 23. A laughing Roosevelt Teddy Bear, with a big smile that shows his teeth, was manufactured to represent Theodore Roosevelt's distinctive robust smile by the Columbia Teddy Bear Co. (Illustration 97) in New York; circa 1907.

Color Illustration 24. Scenes from the book *The Roosevelt Bears Their Travels and Adventures* adorn all four sides of this pitcher, 8in (20cm) tall and 4¾in (12cm) wide, made by Buffalo Pottery, Buffalo, New York, copyright 1906 (actual production year was 1907). *Donna and Keith Kaonis Collection.*

Color Illustration 26. The Roosevelt Bears Rubber Stamps. The colorful scene of the Roosevelt Bears dancing to the music of the hurdy-gurdy man, while the little monkey attempts to collect the money, decorate this box of rubber stamps. Circa 1907, 6in (15cm) long by 4¼in (11cm) wide.

Color Illustration 25. The famous Roosevelt Bear books created by Paul Piper under the pen name Seymour Eaton. The first book, *The Roosevelt Bears, their Travels and Adventures,* was published in 1905. Three more books in this series followed: *More About the Roosevelt Bears* (1906), *The Roosevelt Bears Abroad* (1907) and *The Bear Detectives* (1907). Published by Edward Stern & Company, Inc., Philadelphia. Hardback cover is 8¾in (22cm) by 11¼in (29cm). The follow-up series to the first four volumes of the Roosevelt Bears books by Seymour Eaton were small editions with fewer colored plates.

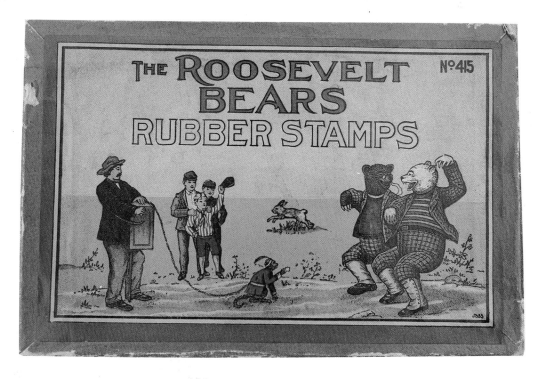

"With outstretched hand and smiling face,
He gave them welcome to the place."

Color Illustration 27. In Seymour Eaton's book *More About Teddy B and Teddy G the Roosevelt Bears*, the adventurous bears visit Washington and are amazed when they are greeted by President Theodore Roosevelt.

Color Illustration 28. Ted E. Bear Goes A-Hunting, a paper cutout. A colorful picture of Ted E. Bear, his clothes, tent and items required for his African hunting trip. "The Start for Africa" is the first of this series. The reverse of the page tells of his adventures. Also advertised is a cutout 20in (51cm) Ted E. Bear (doll) on muslin, to be sewn together and stuffed *(Color Illustration 29)*. In addition, there is a tissue pattern of a separate uniform. Taken from the *Pictorial Review* magazine, circa 1909.

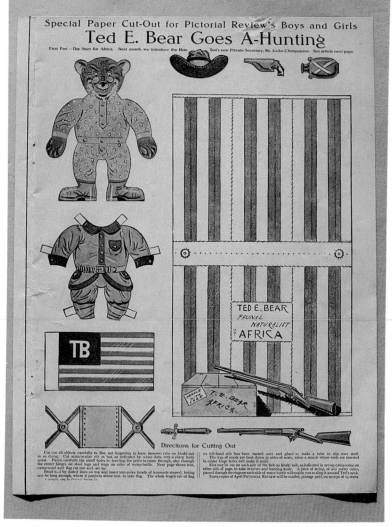

Color Illustration 29. Ted E. Bear cloth doll-bear (advertised on the reverse of Ted E. Bear Goes A-Hunting paper cutout, [*Color Illustration 28*]) in four colors on muslin. To be cut, sewn together and stuffed. The Pictorial Review Company, New York, 1909. This doll is so elusive and rare that many wondered if it had ever been produced. *Beverly Port Collection, photograph by John Paul Port.*

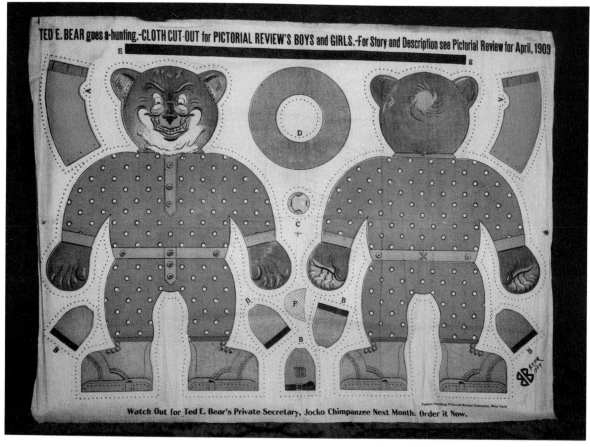

Color Illustration 30. Left: Theodore Roosevelt (Teddy Bear) campaign pin 1904, with 3in (8cm) Teddy Bear made of low quality white plush with black button eyes and unjointed head and body. With Roosevelt's association with the Teddy Bear, political items would use the Teddy Bear. **Right:** Teddy Roosevelt campaign button, 1904, 1¾in (5cm) in diameter. Original pin.

Color Illustration 31. Top: Roosevelt Bears were advertising spokesmen for Teddy Bear Bread. The shape of a gray Roosevelt bear colorfully wearing a red jacket and yellow and red checked trousers and gray sweater is cut out of tin. Circa 1907, 3in (7cm) tall. **Bottom:** Embossed Teddy B and Teddy G decorate this brass bandanna clip. 2½in (6cm) across.

Color Illustration 32. Postcard "Teddy and Rosa on their Way to the White House." Postmarked 1907, C. E. Wheelock and Co., Peoria, Ill. *Mimi Hiscox Collection.*

Color Illustration 33. Heart motif bandanna with Theodore Roosevelt's picture in the center is to highlight Roosevelt receiving the Nobel Peace Prize in 1904 for mediating the Russo-Sino War (see the representatives from those nations pictured at the desk). At the top, Roosevelt is charging up San Juan Hill in the Spanish Civil War. *Richard Friz Collection.*

Color Illustration 34. Right: 13¼in (34cm) by 17in (43cm) oval lithographed tin tray depicting Teddy Roosevelt in Rough Rider uniform on horse with tropical background; border of flags and military motif vignettes. **Left:** 13½in (34cm) by 17in (43cm) oval lithographed tin tray with portrait of Teddy Roosevelt (after John S. Sargent's painting, reproduced by courtesy of *Collier's Weekly,* copyright 1903, *Collier's Weekly,* "The Meek and Beach Co., Coshocton, Ohio"); rose border with Teddy Roosevelt incorporated on either side. *Chick Harris Collection.*

Color Illustration 35. President Theodore Roosevelt appeared on the cover of *TIME* magazine in 1958. The cover portrait was painted by Aaron Bohrod, the great *trompe l'oeil* (fool-the-eye) artist. Bohrod's Roosevelt symbolism alludes to the popular President's square deal policy, gunboat diplomacy, building the Panama canal, his Bull Moose party, his career as a Rough Rider and his "big stick" philosophy. The initials carved in the wood reflect Roosevelt's support of John Muir and the Conservationists. *Courtesy TIME.*

Color Illustration 36. The days of free-wheeling business ethics produced unwitting advertising testimonials from politicians. A tin stand-up display depicts Theodore Roosevelt in full Rough Rider regalia drinking Lemp beer. *Courtesy Richard Friz.*

Color Illustration 37. "Apostle of Prosperity" Theodore Roosevelt Poster. Gustav Fuchs, delineator and publisher, Chicago Carqueville Litho Co., 1903, 15½in (39cm) by 19in (48cm). *Courtesy The New York Historical Society, New York.*

Color Illustration 38. Roosevelt's distinctive facial features and robust smile adorned many items during his adventuresome life. An amusing 1904 mechanical trade card depicts Teddy Roosevelt with his famous mustache which flips up when the string is pulled to reveal a sales message. *Richard Friz Collection.*

Color Illustration 39. 7½in (19cm) Teddy Roosevelt Toby Pitcher (Design by Edward Penfield). Teddy is portrayed in hunting outfit with red bandanna, holding a gun and book; the handle is in the shape of an elephant's head and trunk. *Chick Harris Collection.*

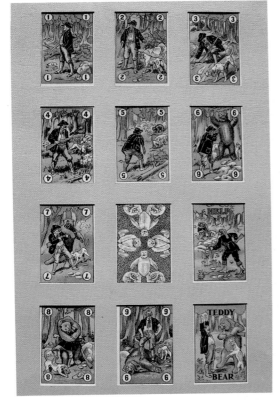

Color Illustration 40. Teddy Roosevelt and the Bear card game. Twelve colorful pictures tell the story of Roosevelt being attacked by a huge grizzly bear during a bear hunt.

Color Illustration 41. Another toy made from a politically derived symbol was Billie Possum (for more information refer to Chapter Seven, "Billie Possum — 'Teddy's Unsuccessful Successor' ").

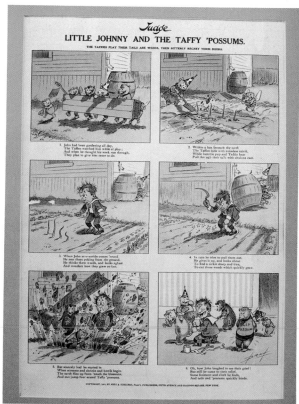

Color Illustration 42. Little Johnny was a familiar sight in the early 1900s *Judge* magazine comic strip, always up to mischief with his friends the "Teddy Bears," (Color Illustration 43). However, when "Billie Possum" came on the scene they made their appearance with Little Johnny in the cartoon but they soon proved an unsuccessful rival for the popular Teddy Bears. The artist of this rare comic strip, "Little Johnny and Taffy Possums," was J. R. Bray. The humorous rhymes were written by Robert D. Towne, published September 11, 1909. *Mimi Hiscox Collection. Photograph by George Hiscox.*

Color Illustration 43. One of the most popular comic strips in 1907 was "Little Johnny and The Teddy Bears," printed by Judge Co., published in their *Judge* magazine in 1907. Later the stories were converted into series of books.

Color Illustration 44. Black bear cubs were often taken from their mothers at an early age to be trained as dancing bears. With their human actions and ability to walk erect on their hind legs they were a natural to amuse and capture the attention of both young and old. *Courtesy American Stock Photos.*

The Three Bears going for a walk.

Irene Peterson.

Color Illustration 45. Many early children's books characterized real bears. One of the most enduring and oldest stories is *The Three Bears*. Raphael Tuck and Sons, New York.

Color Illustration 46. The renown story of *The Three Bears* has been beautifully illustrated over the years by numerous artists. This enchanting picture is a McLoughlin Brothers of New York's rendition.

Mr. Big Bear, Mrs. Middle Bear, and Master Tiny Bear, out for a walk.

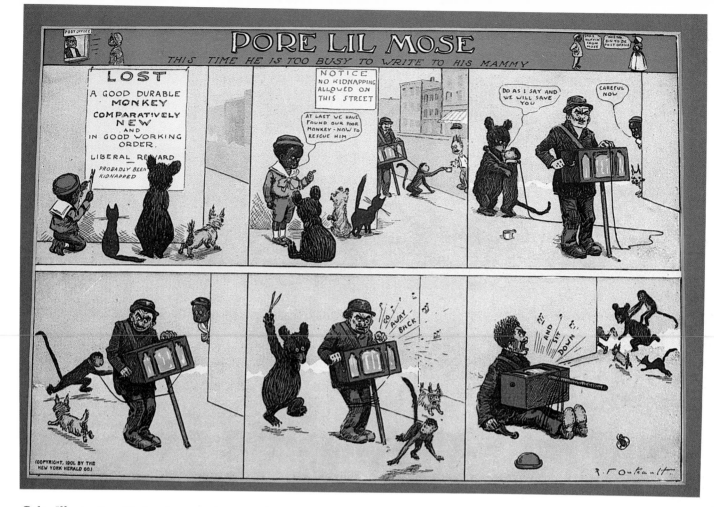

Color Illustration 47. Another popular artist during the beginning of the 20th century was R. F. Outcault, famed for his Buster Brown and dog Tige. Outcault also cartooned a realistic-looking little bear that appeared in the amusing comic strips "Pore Lil Mose" in the *New York Herald,* (copyright 1901 by the New York Herald Co.).

Color Illustration 48. R. F. Outcault's creation of the cute, realistic-looking little bear appeared on a series of valentine postcards in the beginning of the 1900s. Note on the postcard in the bottom left-hand corner the bear is called "Billy."

119

Color Illustration 49. Child's mirror with a picture on the back of Buddy Tucker and a little bear that appears to be R. F. Outcault's creation, Billy; circa 1903. *Mimi Hiscox Collection.*

'Said Freddie to his brother Ted, "I'll play a joke on teacher,
Just watch me for a minute, and you'll see a funny creature;
I'll draw his 'phiz' upon the board; he'll know just how I stand."
But just as he had finished it he felt the teacher's hand.

Color Illustration 50. The Busy Bears book told funny stories in simple words by George W. Gunn, colorfully illustrated in 12 humorous pictures by Austen. This particular illustration of little Freddie's early experience in the field of art is the selfsame amusing incident that happened to Clifford Berryman when he was a young lad *(Illustration 1).*

THE LITTLE BEARS HAVE TO LEARN DIFFICULT FEATS.

Color Illustration 51. Because of the popularity of the bear and the way they simulate human activities in every conceivable way, they were a natural subject for talented artists to caricature. The story of *The Little Bears* by Fredrika Groosvenor, is a tale of two mischievous little bears, colorfully illustrated, copyright 1905, McLoughlin Brothers, New York.

Chapter Eight

Theodore Roosevelt —
"The Man of His Youthful Dreams"

Illustration 129. Theodore Roosevelt (or "Teedie" as his family called him) about the age of four. *Courtesy Theodore Roosevelt Collection, Harvard College Library.*

Illustration 130. The house in which Theodore Roosevelt was born at 28 East Twentieth Street, New York, was a narrow five-story, rather gloomy-style building. Photograph copyright International Film Service from *The Life of Theodore Roosevelt* by W. M. Draper Lewis, copyright 1919 by W. M. Ellis Scull.

Theodore Roosevelt, a hero to millions of Americans, was the youngest and most popular President of the United States since George Washington.

Born October 27, 1858, in a rather gloomy house in New York City, he was raised in the protective shelter of a prosperous well-established family of Dutch importers. His father was a large, kind man. His mother was a sweet, gracious woman from an aristocratic Georgian family, who told young Teedie (as his family called him) romantic stories of the old South.

He was born a sickly child, suffering from frightening attacks of agonizing asthma. His father would take him for long drives in his open carriage until his breathing spasms subsided, or force him to drink black coffee or smoke cigars, a late 19th century cure incredibly proclaimed to induce vomiting and cease the violent asthma attacks.

Due to Teedie's ill health he was unable to attend boarding school (as was fashionable for children of his social stature) and he had to be educated by tutors. He gave few signs pointing to a very exceptional future, but he was "plucky and persevering."

At age seven, Teedie was a budding zoologist. In his teens he studied taxidermy, collecting birds, insects, snakes and mice. Through boyhood he carried the smell of arsenic used to cure the skins of animals.

Young Roosevelt discovered his inevitable need for spectacles when he could hardly hit a thing with his father's gift of a 12-gauge double-barreled shotgun in the summer of 1872. Reminiscing, he wrote years later, "I had no idea how beautiful the world was...I could not see, and yet was wholly ignorant that I was not seeing."

As a youth he had a passion for reading and entertained himself with books on travel and adventure. Throughout his phenomenal life he wrote 34 books on history, nature and political philosophy. He even dictated one while shaving.

As he grew older his health began to improve. To encourage his frail son to develop his physical health and appearance, his father installed a gymnasium on the back piazza of the house, giving him challenging words of warning: "You have the mind, but you haven't got the body. To do all you can with your mind, you must make your body match it." In time the determined young lad grew into a robust and healthy man.

In 1876 he was enrolled as a freshman and entered the University of Harvard. Weighing 125 pounds, he was now as tall as he would grow, five feet eight inches. Having an almost comical falsetto break in his voice he still became a brilliant public speaker. He was always ready to join anything. Barred from baseball and football because of his poor eyesight, he turned his attention to becoming an excellent boxer.

Teddy (as he was later affectionately nicknamed) loved the great outdoors and taught himself to be an excellent horseback rider and hunting sportsman. He became proficient in the art of hunting bear. He had a tremendous endurance, riding 100 miles on horseback in a single day. For him, two weeks of bear hunting was relaxation.

Although he was remembered as a great hunter, Roosevelt loved animals and nature. His passion for hunting bear in particular was not solely to kill them but to observe their natural habits. The grizzly bears became his favorites.

Re-elected President in 1904 by the greatest popular majority ever, he elatedly told his wife, "I am no longer a political accident." (Roosevelt became President upon the assassination of McKinley in 1901.)

This great statesman's face is carved on the side of South Dakota's Mount Rushmore in recognition of his efforts on behalf of conservation. He also organized the Rough Riders, made possible the Panama Canal and established the National Parks system.

He was a many-sided character, but all sides were good. He believed in the "strenuous life" and demanded that America "lives up to its great mission in the world." He said, "Keep your eyes on the stars but your feet on the ground." People loved him. He was amusing, entertaining and always laughed loudly at this own jokes. "Delighted" was one of the President's famous expressions.

He was known for his favorite descriptive expression — "bully." In foreign affairs he met with success after success by "speaking softly and carrying a big

Illustration 131. Theodore Roosevelt as a student at Harvard. Photograph copyright International Film Service from *The Life of Theodore Roosevelt* by W. M. Draper Lewis, copyright 1919 by W. M. Ellis Scull.

stick," while preserving world peace. He gave and insisted on the "square deal" and "fair play."

When he became the first President and first American to win the Nobel Peace Prize, he gave the prize money to charity.

Teddy Roosevelt was also the first President to fly an airplane. Since the earliest flights of the Wright Brothers, he had been fascinated by aircrafts. On October 11, 1910, during a St. Louis Air Meet held at Kinloch Field, Roosevelt was invited to ride in an early biplane that was little more than wings and an open frame. Without hesitating he accepted. Wearing only a business suit and goggles, he was strapped into the aircraft.

As he descended from his three-minute and twenty-second flight, the delighted president described the flight as "bully" *(Illustration 146)*.

Roosevelt adored children and was a devoted father. His was a new type of presidential family, close and affectionate. Their activities often took precedence over affairs of state.

His six active children are said to have roller-skated in the White House ballroom, rode a pony in the elevator and dropped huge snowballs on the guards. Spending time with his children was an important and necessary part of Roosevelt's day. He clearly loved to

take them for long tramps through the woods. These events were to the children like "voyages into the unknown." He would entertain them for hours around a campfire with horrifying ghost stories. A favorite game he played with them was the game of bear. The children pretended they were big game hunters, while their father acted the part of the ferocious animal. Christmas to Teddy as a child was "an occasion of literally delirious joy." It was an annual pleasure for Roosevelt to reproduce the joys of his youth for his own children.

When away from home, the busy President would find time to write to his children, illustrating his letters with humorous sketches. Included in the book *Theodore Roosevelt's Letters to His Children* (Charles Scribner's Sons, New York, 1919) is an illustrated letter the President wrote to his son, Archie, on October 16, 1907:

"Dear Archie:

"We have had no luck with the bear; but we have killed as many deer as we needed for meat, and the hounds caught a wildcat. Our camp is

The Rough-Rider of 1898

Illustration 132. Colonel Theodore Roosevelt of the Rough Riders. In 1898, as a devoted leader, Roosevelt trained his regiment, the "Rough Riders" (the first U.S. volunteer cavalry), and led them into battle during the Spanish-American War. Photograph copyright 1910 by Underwood and Underwood. *Courtesy Bettman Archives.*

Illustration 133. A youthful hunting picture of Theodore Roosevelt from *The Life of Theodore Roosevelt* by W. M. Draper Lewis, copyright 1919 by W. M. Ellis Scull. Roosevelt's skill with a rifle developed during his hunting days in the West.

as comfortable as possible, and we have great camp fires at night. One of the bear-hunting planters with me told me he once saw a bear, when overtaken by hounds, lie down flat on its back with all its legs stretched out, while the dogs barked furiously all around it.

"Suddenly the bear sat up with a jump, and frightened all the dogs so that they nearly turned back somersaults.

"At this camp there is a nice tame pussycat which lies out here all the time, catching birds, mice, or lizards; but very friendly with any party of hunters which happens along.

"P.S. I have just killed a bear; I have written Kermit about it."

Roosevelt illustrated the amusing story with two sketches *(Illustration 139).*

Through his delight in his own children, young Americans were also drawn towards the kind, chivalrous President. His great friend, Jacob A. Riis, said of him:

"Boys admire President Roosevelt because he, himself, is a good deal of a boy. Some men have claimed that Mr. Roosevelt never has matured; but this is saying no more than that he has not stopped growing, that he is not yet imprisoned in the crust of age. To him the world is still young and unfinished. He has a boy's fresh faith that the things that ought to be done can be done. His eyes are on the future rather than on the past.

"Young Americans never drew so near to any other public man as Theodore Roosevelt. All the boys in the land feel that there is a kindred spirit in the White House. Every one of them knows 'Teddy' and the 'Teddy Bear' and the 'Teddy Hat'. But it is doubtful if the President ever was called 'Teddy' when he was a boy. He used to be 'Teedy' in the family circle and at Harvard he was 'Ted', while among the intimates of his manhood he is always called 'Theodore'. He is 'Teddy' Roosevelt to millions of boys who delight in their comradeship with the President which this nickname implies. It does not mean that they are lacking in respect for him; it simply means that they are not afraid of him, and that they feel they know him and he knows them."

Illustration 134. Roosevelt as a cowboy from *The Life of Theodore Roosevelt* by W. M. Draper Lewis, copyright 1919 by Wm. Ellis Scull. Roosevelt's great strength and fine health was gained from his early days at Chimney Butte and Elkhorn ranches in Dakota where he gained a reputation for fearless and square dealing.

PRESIDENT ROOSEVELT AND FAMILY

Illustration 135. President Roosevelt with his family at Sagamore Hill, Oyster Bay, Long Island, 1903.

READY FOR THE FESTIVITIES.

Illustration 136. "Ready for the Festivites." *The Washington Post,* March 4, 1905. Uncle Sam makes ready for Theodore Roosevelt's Inaugural Ball. Berryman's Bear is splendidly dressed for the occasion in his smart Rough Rider outfit. *Richard Friz Collection.*

Illustration 137. Clifford Berryman's magnificent cartoon of President Theodore Roosevelt's inaugural ball of March 4, 1905, was published in a special inauguration section of *The Washington Post*, March 5, 1905, on pages two and three. The drawing was about five times the size of the regular front page cartoon. Unable to miss the historical festivities was a clandestine guest. Hiding in the shadows of the impressive looking pillars, among the numerous portraits and rendering of the lavish background, enjoying the exceeding grandeur of the occasion was the outline of the President's faithful little friend — the Teddy Bear. *Courtesy Library of Congress.*

Illustration 138. Uncle Sam says: "He's good enough for me!" The striking cartoon on this political postcard, drawn by Homer Davenport, became the most prominent campaign document of the Republican party in 1904. *Bernard Greenhouse Collection.*

The Bear Plays Dead

The Bear Sits Up

Illustration 139. When away from home, President Roosevelt would find time to write to his children illustrating his letters with humorous sketches. In a letter to his son, Archie, he illustrated the story of a bear hunt where the bear played dead when overtaken by hounds. Then suddenly the bear sat up with a jump, and frightened all the dogs so that they nearly turned somersaults. *Courtesy Charles Scribner's Sons.*

Illustration 140. Theodore Roosevelt adored children and was a devoted father. His family life was a model for the American people. Copyright by Underwood and Underwood. *Courtesy Bettman Archives.*

Illustration 141. "The President in Panama." Roosevelt's little companion takes a sneak preview of the work on the Panama Canal through the President's binoculars. *Courtesy Library of Congress.*

Illustration 142. "Will He Knock It Out?" The little Teddy Bear cannot bear to watch the President enforcing his philosophy: "Speak Softly But Carry A Big Stick," (1908). *Courtesy Library of Congress.*

"Had Theodore Roosevelt had his way, there would be no Christmas trees today. But why would our 26th president want to do away with Christmas trees?

"In the early 1900s, Roosevelt was certain that the cutting of Christmas trees amounted to the looting of the nation's forests. Allowing such a thing to continue, he was sure it would mean certain ruin for some of this nation's beautiful scenery.

"During his re-election campaign of 1904, he made several promises, one of them had been to conserve natural resources. To prove he was a man of his word, he forbade the use of Christmas trees in the White House. While he had no power to stop the selling of trees, he asked the people of this country to follow his lead and not buy Christmas trees.

"The sale of Christmas trees did decline, and Roosevelt was pleased with this turn of events. His happiness, however, was short-lived, because he soon discovered that his own sons, Archie and Quintin [sic], didn't care for his idea.

"The boys said it wouldn't be Christmas without a tree. Thus they defied their father, and set up a tree in Archie's room.

"The president was furious, and ordered the tree be taken down. But the boys had anticipated his reaction. They had already approached Gifford Pinchot, a well-known conservationist of the time, and learned that he wasn't against Christmas trees.

"Pinchot, a man whom Roosevelt respected explained to the president that conservation didn't mean to prohibit tree cutting, but to be selective about where and what was being cut. He explained further that he was convinced that the cutting and thinning of trees actually helped the forest growth.

"Although there had been uncontrolled cutting of all trees, not just Christmas trees, modern forestry techniques were now being used, Pinchot said. When trees were cut down, new trees were planted so the forests could replenish themselves.

"Additionally, when forests are not thinned periodically, new trees cannot grow because of insufficient sunlight and moisture.

"Apparently Pinchot did a good job of convincing Roosevelt to modify his view on Christmas trees. Roosevelt didn't rescind his plea not to buy Christmas trees that year, but he did let Archie and Quintin [sic] keep their tree. That next year, the White House once again had a magnificent Christmas tree.

"Fortunately, the cutting of Christmas trees has become less of a problem. Today, most trees are not taken from forests but are grown on tree farms."

Illustration 143. "Save The Forests!" was on page 3 of *The Evening Star* on December 8, 1908. Uncle Sam, with the help of Berryman's enthusiastic little bear, inspires Americans to plant more trees and save the existing forests, enforcing Roosevelt's conservation and natural resource laws. The following article by Richard Bauman, published in the December 1986 edition of the *Fedco Reporter* tells the story: "When Teddy Nearly Ruined Christmas."

In 1909 Theodore Roosevelt was authorized by the Smithsonian Institution to head a scientific expedition in Africa to obtain animal and plant specimens for the National Museum at Washington, D.C. After the inauguration ceremonies of William Taft, Roosevelt left by train to the shouts of "Goodbye Teddy" to begin the 12-month hunting trip. Accompanying Roosevelt as his fellow members of the expedition were his son, Kermit (who acted as the photographer of the party); American naturalists: Mr. J. Alden Loring, Lieutenant-Colonel A. Mearns, Mr. Edmund Heller; and two British experts on African hunting: Mr. Cunningham and Mr. Tarlton.

Over 11,000 specimens were received for the National Museum, including approximately 5000 mammals (most of them large), nearly 4000 birds and a great number of reptiles and smaller creatures.

Roosevelt's association with his fellow creatures had always been humane and never cruel. For the most part, he hunted in the interest of science and collected rare animals (with the exception of the lion which are considered vermin in South Africa). Roosevelt wrote an account of his African experiences and achievements in his notable volume *African Game Trials*.

After a serious illness Theodore Roosevelt died peacefully in his sleep at his home in Sagamore Hill, Oyster Bay, Long Island, on January 6, 1919, at the age of 60.

It was said "death had to take him sleeping or there would have been a fight."

Senator Johnson of California, friend and running mate of Roosevelt in 1912 said in his memorial on January 6, 1919:

"The greatest American of our generation has passed away. He had a truer vision, a higher courage, a wiser statesmanship than any man of our time. I cannot speak of him in ordinary terms. To me he had no parallel — none approached him in virility or force or profound knowledge of varied subjects. He stood alone in greatness of perception, in courage for the right as he saw it. I am mourning not only the greatest American, a world figure such as time seldom presents, but a thoughtful, kindly, affectionate friend."

Theodore Roosevelt will long be remembered as the boy who "grew up to be the man of his youthful dreams."

The Teddy Roosevelt Association has been formed in honor of this national hero. A non-profit organization chartered by Congress in 1920, they invite you to join to help perpetuate the memory and ideals of Teddy Roosevelt. They are an historical association and public service group, with members throughout the United States. They publish and disseminate the Teddy Roosevelt Association Journal. Published four times a year, the Journal is available by writing to: Teddy Roosevelt Association, Box 720, Oyster Bay, Long Island, New York 11771.

Illustration 144. "Christmas 1912." *Courtesy Smithsonian Institution.*

Illustration 145. "The Senate Committee on Library is Embarrassed by the Necessity of Choosing Between Rival Busts of Theodore Roosevelt as Vice President, for the Senate Chamber." The inquisitive little bear is seen peering over Uncle Sam's shoulder asking him, "What makes 'em so quiet, Uncle?" Original. *In the Collection of the Corcoran Gallery of Art, gift of the artist.*

Illustration 147. "Christmas At the White House," *Judge* magazine, from the book *A Cartoon History of Roosevelt's Career* by Albert Shaw, copyright 1910 by the Review of Reviews Company. *Courtesy Toby Roberts.*

Illustration 146. Teddy Roosevelt was the first President to fly on an airplane. Since the earliest flights of the Wright Brothers, he had been fascinated by aircraft. On October 11, 1910, during a St. Louis Air Meet held at Kinloch Field, Roosevelt accepted an invitation to ride in an early biplane that was no more than wings and an open frame. *Courtesy Smithsonian Institution.*

Illustration 148. Roosevelt says: "Oh this is bully! Just think of poor Taft back home wrestling with Congress," *The News Tribune* (Duluth) from the book *A Cartoon History of Roosevelt's Career* by Albert Shaw, copyright 1910 by The Review of Reviews Company. *Courtesy Toby Roberts.*

Illustration 149. "Meeting of Sovereigns in the Center of Africa. His Majesty, the King of the Desert: 'In the name of that Nobel whose prize covers you with glory, O Teddy, I implore you to spare other thousands of my subjects,' " Pasgino (Turin) from the book *A Cartoon History of Roosevelt's Career* by Albert Shaw, copyright 1910 by The Review of Reviews Company. *Courtesy Toby Roberts.*

Illustration 150. "Theodorus Africanus," *The World* (New York), from the book *A Cartoon History of Roosevelt's Career* by Albert Shaw, copyright 1910 by The Review of Reviews Company. Roosevelt gathering specimens for the Smithsonian Institution during his African expedition in 1909. *Courtesy Toby Roberts.*

Illustration 151. "Bwana Tumbo" (means Big Chief) was the name given to Roosevelt by the African natives. From the book *African Game Trails*, by Theodore Roosevelt. Copyright 1909, 1910 by Charles Scribners' Sons. *Courtesy Shirley Tisch.*

A Chronology of Theodore Roosevelt

1858 — Born October 27 at 28 East 20th Street, New York City.

1880 — Graduated from Harvard; married Alice Hathaway Lee on October 27.

1882 to 1884 — Member of New York State Assembly.

1882 — Published *Naval War of 1812*, first of many books on history, nature, travel and public affairs.

1884 — Death of Alice Lee Roosevelt on February 14.

1884 to 1886 — Rancher in Dakota Territory.

1886 — Unsuccessful candidate for Mayor of New York City; married Edith Kermit Carrow on December 2.

1889 to 1895 — Appointed U.S. Civil Service Commissioner.

1895 to 1897 — Commissioner, New York City Police Board.

1897 to 1898 — Assistant Secretary of the Navy.

1898 — Organized Rough Riders.

1898 to 1901 — Governor of State of New York.

1901 — Vice President of the United States; becomes President September 14, on the death of McKinley; began policy of "trust busting" in 1901.

1902 — Began vigorous conservation program.

1903 — Directs negotiations for the Panama Canal Zone.

1904 — Elected President of the United States on November 8.

1905 — Brought Russia and Japan to peace table at Portsmouth, New Hampshire.

1906 — Pure Food and Drug Act passed for consumer protection.

1909 to 1910 — Hunted big game in Africa.

1910 — Received Nobel Peace Prize in Oslo, Norway.

1909 to 1914 — Contributing editor of *The Outlook* magazine.

1912 — Unsuccessful Progressive (Bull Moose) Party candidate for President.

1914 — Explored "River of Doubt" in jungles of Brazil.

1914 to 1917 — Prominent advocate of American preparedness and intervention in World War I.

1919 — Died at home, Sagamore Hill, Oyster Bay, Long Island, on January 6.

Chapter Nine

The 1900s in the Louisiana Canebrakes
by Theodore Roosevelt

Illustration 152. On his second bear hunt in the Delta, Mississippi, area, President Theodore Roosevelt arrived on the Belle of the Bends boat in 1907. *Courtesy Old Court House Museum, Vicksburg, Mississippi.*

The following article, written during President Roosevelt's second term in the White House, was published in *Scribner's Magazine* in January 1908. The President describes in great detail his 1907 successful Louisiana bear hunt.

"In October, 1907, I spent a fortnight in the canebrakes of northern Louisiana, my hosts being Messrs. John M. Parker and John A. McIlhenny. Surgeon-General Rixey, of the United States Navy, and Doctor Alexander Lambert were with me. I was especially anxious to kill a bear in these canebrakes after the fashion of the old southern planters, who for a century past have followed the bear in Louisiana, Mississippi, and Arkansas.

"Our first camp was on Tensas Bayou. This is in the heart of the great alluvial bottom-land created during the countless ages through which the mighty Mississippi has poured out the heart of the continent...

"The canebrakes stretch along the slight rises of ground, often extending for miles, forming one of the most striking and interesting features of the country. They choke out other growths, the feathery, graceful canes standing in ranks, tall, slender, serried, each but a few inches from his brother, and springing to a height of fifteen or twenty feet. They look like bamboos; they are well-nigh impenetrable to a man on horseback; even on foot they make difficult walking unless free use is made of the heavy bush-knife.

"It is impossible to see through them for more than fifteen or twenty paces, and often for not half that distance. Bears make their lairs in them, and they are the refuge for hunted things. Outside of them, in the swamp, bushes of many kinds grow thick among the tall trees, and vines and creepers climb the trunks and hang in trailing festoons from the branches. Here, likewise, the bush-knife is in constant play, as the skilled horsemen thread their way, often at a great gallop, in and out among the great tree trunks, and through the dense, tangled, thorny undergrowth.

"At our first camp our tents were pitched by the bayou. For four days the weather was hot, with steaming rains; after that it grew cool and clear. Huge biting flies, bigger than bees, attacked our horses; but the insect plagues, so veritable a scourge in this country during the months of warm weather, had well-nigh vanished in the first few weeks of the fall.

"The morning after we reached camp we

Illustration 153. The Old Court House Museum in Vicksburg, Mississippi, constructed in 1858, now reflects treasures from its southern heritage. On the top floor of the museum is this wonderful exhibit of rare items representing President Theodore Roosevelt's 1902 and 1907 visits to the area to hunt bear. In the right-hand corner of the case the following report is given about Roosevelt's 1907 visit: "Roosevelt Came Again in 1907." "Thousands of people crowded Court Square in Vicksburg on October 21, 1907 to hear President Theodore Roosevelt on his second trip to Mississippi. The entire city was decorated with flags and bunting 'Roosevelt Day' and delegations from throughout the state were in attendance to hear him speak including a group who held a banner aloft asking that he send the battleship, Mississippi Natchez, to receive her silver service. Throngs met the steamboat on which he travelled, The Belle of the Bends, and hosts included Confederate General Stephen Dill Lee. Though Roosevelt was a Republican, the young Democrats welcomed the President with Banners and the presidential parade passed beneath an arch made of cotton bales on Main Street enroute to the Old Court House. Roosevelt was so impressed with the city that he later sent his wife and children here on vacation. The President began his speech with praise for Warren County's favorite son, Conferderate Pres. Jefferson Davis, a man he had once severely criticized. The applause was thunderous. Margaret Davis Hayes of Colorado Springs, daughter of the Southern Leader, wrote to President Roosevelt, 'There are very few men with real courage enough to say "I have made a mistake and wish to make amends" and when I see such a man he commands my admiration and respect.'" *Courtesy Old Court House Museum, Vicksburg, Mississippi.*

were joined by Ben Lilley, the hunter, a spare, full-bearded man, with wild, gentle, blue eyes and a frame of steel and whipcord. I never met any other man so indifferent to fatigue and hardship. He equalled Cooper's Deerslayer in woodcraft, in hardihood, in simplicity — and also in loquacity. The morning he joined us in camp, he had come on foot through the thick woods, followed by his two dogs, and had neither eaten nor drunk for twenty-four hours; for he did not like to drink the swamp water. It had rained hard throughout the night and he had no shelter, no rubber coat, nothing but the clothes he was wearing, and the ground was too wet for him to lie on; so he perched in a crooked tree in the beating rain, much as if he had been a wild turkey. But he was not in the least tired when he struck camp; and, though he slept an hour after breakfast, it was chiefly because he had nothing else to do, inasmuch as it was Sunday, on which day he never hunted nor labored.

"Late in the evening of the same day we were joined by two gentlemen, to whom we owed the success of our hunt. They were Messrs. Clive and Harley Metcalf, planters from Mississippi, men in the prime of life, thorough woodsmen and hunters, skilled marksmen, and utterly fearless horsemen. For a quarter of a century they had hunted bear and deer with horse and hound, and were masters of the art. They brought with them their pack of bear hounds, only one, however, being a thoroughly staunch and seasoned veteran.

"The pack was under the immediate control of a negro hunter, Holt Collier, in his own way as remarkable a character as Ben Lilley...

"When ten years old Holt had been taken on the horse behind his young master, the Hinds of that day, on a bear hunt, when he killed his first bear. In the Civil War he had not only followed his master to battle as his body-servant, but had acted under him as sharpshooter against the Union soldiers. After the war he continued to stay with his master until the latter died, and had then been adopted by the Metcalfs; and he felt that he had brought them up, and treated them with that mixture of affection and grumbling respect which an old nurse shows toward the lad who has ceased being a child. The two Metcalfs and Holt understood one another thoroughly, and understood their hounds and the game their hounds followed almost as thoroughly.

"They had killed many deer and wildcat, and now and then a panther; but their favorite game was the black bear, which, until within a very few years, was extraordinarily plentiful in the swamps and canebrakes on both sides of the

"HE'S GONE!"
Celebration in the Cane Brakes.

Cartoon in the New Orleans Times-Democrat the day after Roosevelt went back to Washington in 190?

Illustration 154. The cartoon "'He's Gone' Celebration in the Cane Brakes," was featured in *The New Orleans Times — Democrat* the day after Roosevelt went back to Washington, D.C., in 1907. *Courtesy Old Court House Museum, Vicksburg, Mississippi.*

lower Mississippi, and which is still found here and there, although in greatly diminished numbers. In Louisiana and Mississippi the bears go into their dens toward the end of January, usually in hollow trees, but often also in great logs that lie rotting on the ground. They come forth toward the end of April, the cubs having been born in the interval. At this time the bears are nearly as fat, so my informants said, as when they enter their dens in January; but they lose their fat very rapidly. On first coming out in the spring they usually eat ash buds and the tender young cane called mutton cane, and at that season they generally refuse to eat the acorns even when they are plentiful. According to my informants it is at this season that they are most apt to take to killing stock, almost always the hogs which run wild or semi-wild in the woods. They are very individual in their habits, however; many of them never touch stock, while others, usually old he-bears, may kill numbers of hogs; in one case an old he-bear began this hog killing just as soon as he left his den.

Illustration 155. When President Theodore Roosevelt visited Vicksburg in 1907, little Homer Smith (left) presented him with a bouquet of flowers. Upon returning to Washington, the President sent a Teddy Bear (Illustration 156) to Homer, but the President mistook the pretty child with long blonde curls for a girl and wrote requesting the Teddy Bear be given to the "dear little girl." *Courtesy Old Court House Museum, Vicksburg, Mississippi.*

"In the summer months they find but little to eat, and it is at this season that they are most industrious in hunting for grubs, insects, frogs, and small mammals. In some neighborhoods they do not eat fish, while in other places, perhaps not far away, they not only greedily eat dead fish, but will themselves kill fish if they can find them in shallow pools left by the receding waters. As soon as the mast is on the ground they begin to feed upon it, and when the acorns and pecans are plentiful they eat nothing else, though at first berries of all kinds and grapes are eaten also. When in November they have begun only to eat the acorns they put on fat as no other wild animal does, and by the end of December a full-grown bear may weigh at least twice as much as it does in August, the difference being as great as between a very fat and a lean hog. Old he-bears which in August weigh three hundred pounds and upwards will, toward the end of December, weigh six hundred pounds, and even more in exceptional cases.

"A big bear is cunning, and is a dangerous fighter to the dogs. It is only in exceptional cases, however, that these black bears, even when wounded and at bay, are dangerous to men, in spite of their formidable strength. Each of the hunters with whom I was camped had been charged by one or two among the scores or hundreds of bears he had slain, but no one of them had ever been injured, although they knew other men who had been injured. Their immunity was due to their own skill and coolness; for when the dogs were around the bear the hunter invariably ran close in so as to kill the bear at once and save the pack.

"For several days we hunted perseveringly around this camp on the Tensas Bayou, but without success...

"A few days convinced us that it was a waste of time to stay longer where we were. Accordingly, early one morning we hunters started for a new camp fifteen or twenty miles to the southward, on Bear Lake...

"From our new camp we hunted as steadily as from the old...

"We had seen the tracks of an old she (she bear) in the neighborhood, and the next morning we started to hunt her out. I went with Clive Metcalf. We had been joined overnight by Mr. Ichabod Osborn and his son Tom, two Louisiana planters, with six or eight hounds — or rather bear dogs, for in these packs most of the animals are of mixed blood, and, as with all packs that are used in the genuine hunting of the wilderness, pedigree counts for nothing as compared with steadiness, courage, and intelligence.

"On reaching the cypress slough near which the tracks of the old she had been seen the day before, Clive Metcalf and I separated from the others and rode off at a lively pace between two of the canebrakes. After an hour or two's wait we heard, very far off, the notes of one of the loudest-mouthed hounds, and instantly rode toward it, until we could make out the babel of the pack. Some hard galloping brought us opposite the point toward which they were heading — for experienced hunters can often tell the probable line of a bear's flight, and the spots at which it will break cover. But on this occasion the bear shied off from leaving the thick cane and doubled back; and soon the hounds were once more out of hearing, while we galloped desperately around the edge of the cane. The tough woods-horses kept their feet like cats as they leaped logs, plunged through bushes, and dodged in and out among the tree trunks; and we had all we could do to prevent the vines from lifting us out of the saddle, while the thorns tore our hands and faces. Hither and

Illustration 156. This wonderful old Teddy Bear was presented to Homer Smith *(Illustration 155)* by President Theodore Roosevelt in 1907. The bear was given to the museum by Mrs. Homer (Lillian) Smith in 1983. *Courtesy Old Court House Museum, Vicksburg, Mississippi.*

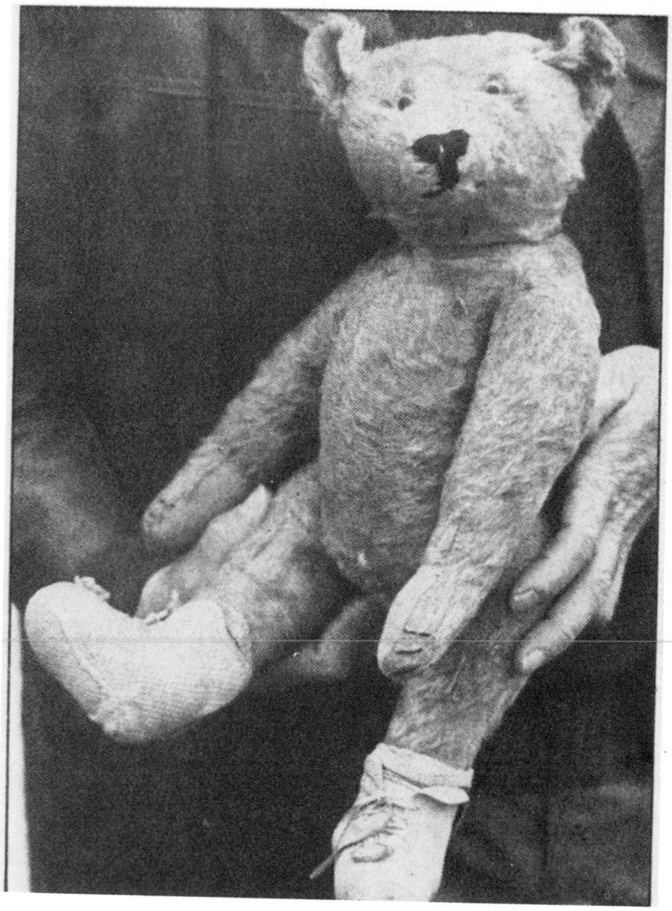

thither we went, now at a trot, now at a run, now stopping to listen for the pack.

"Occasionally we could hear the hounds, and then off we would go racing through the forest toward the point for which we thought they were heading. Finally, after a couple of hours of this, we came up on one side of a canebrake on the other side of which we could hear, not only the pack, but the yelling and cheering of Harley Metcalf and Tom Osborn and one or two of the negro hunters, all of whom were trying to keep the dogs up to their work in the thick cane. Again we rode ahead, and now in a few minutes were rewarded by hearing the leading dogs come to bay in the thickest of the cover. Having galloped as near to the spot as we could we threw ourselves off the horses and plunged into the cane, trying to cause as little disturbance as possible, but of course utterly unable to avoid making some noise. Before we were within gunshot, however, we could tell by the sounds that the bear had once again started, making what is called a 'walking bay.'

"Clive Metcalf, a finished bear-hunter, was speedily able to determine what the bear's probable course would be, and we stole through the cane until we came to a spot near which he thought the quarry would pass. Then we crouched down, I with my rifle at the ready. Nor did we have long to wait. Peering through the thick-growing stalks I suddenly made out the dim outline of the bear coming straight toward us; and noiselessly I cocked and half-raised my rifle, waiting for a clearer chance. In a few seconds it came; the bear turned almost broadside to me, and walked forward very stiff-legged, almost as if on tiptoe, now and then looking back at the nearest dogs. These were two in number — Rowdy, a very deep-voiced hound, in the lead, and Queen, a shrill-tongued brindled bitch, a little behind. Once or twice the bear paused as she looked back at them, evidently hoping that they would come so near that she could catch one of them. But they were too wary.

"All of this took but a few moments, and as I saw the bear quite distinctly some twenty yards off, I fired for behind the shoulder. Although I could see her outline, yet the cane was so thick that my sight was on it and not on the bear itself. But I knew my bullet would go true; and, sure enough, at the crack of the rifle the bear stumbled and fell forward...slain in the canebrake in true hunter fashion...

"Then we dragged the bear out to the edge of the cane, and my companion wound his horn to summon the other hunters. This was a big she-bear, very lean, and weighing two hundred and two pounds....

"After the death of my bear I had only a couple of days left. We spent them a long distance from camp, having to cross two bayous before we got to the hunting grounds. I missed a shot at a deer, seeing little more than the flicker of its white tail through the dense bushes; and the pack caught and killed a very lean two-year-old bear weighing eighty pounds. Near a beautiful pond called Panther Lake we found a deer-lick, the ground not merely bare, but furrowed into hollows by the tongues of the countless generations of deer that had frequented the place. We also passed a huge mound, and only hillock in the entire district; it was the work of man, for it had been built in the unknown past by those unknown people whom we call mound-builders. On the trip, all told, we killed and brought into camp three bear, six deer, a wild-cat, a turkey, a possum, and a dozen squirrels...."

Illustration 157. "Think of what may be." *Courtesy Library of Congress.*

Illustration 158. "President Roosevelt Finds the Denizens of The Canebrakes Prepared," *The Herald* (New York), from the book *A Cartoon History of Roosevelt's Career* by Albert Shaw, copyright 1910 by The Review of Reviews Company. Theodore Roosevelt's courageous and eventful life was caricatured by many political cartoonists of the day. *Courtesy Toby Roberts.*

Chapter Ten

Holt Collier — Teddy Roosevelt's Guide

Born in Greenville, Mississippi, on January 21, 1846, Holt Collier (*Illustration 159*) achieved great distinction as a big game hunter. He guided President Roosevelt on his South Delta and Louisiana bear hunts.

Collier was responsible for capturing the bear Roosevelt refused to shoot during the famous 1902 Mississippi bear hunt. In relating this memorable incident, Collier said, "The President of the United States was anxious to see a live bear the first day of the hunt. I told him he would see that bear if I had to tie it and bring it to him." Before the end of the first day Collier, with the aid of his famous pack of trained hounds, made good his word.

Upon his return to Washington, Roosevelt sent Holt a rifle, duplicating the one used on the hunt and admired by Holt.

Collier was a remarkable character. An ex-slave and Confederate soldier, he was devoted to his master, Howell Hinds, who bought him when he was only seven years old.

Holt's training to be a great hunter and marksman began when he was ten. At that time his master bought him a 12-gauge shotgun. Stationed on the porch of a cabin in the slave quarters, Hinds gave him instructions to shoot the blackbirds that swarmed over the chinaberry trees, so that the cook in the "big house" could make blackbird pie. During the next few years the young hunter gained the respect of his master. Their relationship became so close that Hinds never went hunting without his devoted friend.

When Holt was 12, he was sent to school with his master's sons to Bardstown, Kentucky. His boyish spirit of adventure and love of hunting caused him to play "hooky" from school. Often hiding his gun in the springhouse, he would slip away into the fields and woods to hunt instead of studying with the other children.

Unsuccessful as Mr. Hinds was at educating the high-spirited young lad, he did manage to teach him to be honorable, truthful and trustworthy. Holt lived by these rules the rest of his life.

Holt traveled with his master in the capacity of juvenile valet. They traveled back and forth to the old home in Jefferson County, to New Orleans to Louisville and to Cincinnati. The main means of travel was by boat.

When the Civil War began, Mr. Hinds and his son joined the Confederate army. Although young Holt, then 14, begged and begged to go with them, his master told him he was too young to enter the army. As Hinds and his son departed they left the disappointed young boy sitting on the fence crying.

Undaunted, the determined lad became a stowaway on the Mississippi River steamship carrying his beloved master off to the war. When Holt was discovered, Mr. Hinds told his son, "Thomas, if we both go to the devil that boy will have to go along!" To which Holt replied, "I've got as good a chance as you."

President Roosevelt wrote about Collier in *Scribner's Magazine* in 1908 in an article entitled "In the Louisiana Canebrakes:"

"He was a man of sixty and could neither read or write, but he had all the dignity of an African chief, and for half a century he had been a bear hunter, having killed or assisted in killing over three thousand bears."

Speaking of his early life in an interview before he died, Holt said, "I am black, but my association with my old Colonel (Mr. Hinds) gave me many advantages. I was freer than I have ever been since. I loved him better than anybody else in the world and would have given my life for him," as tears rolled down his withered old cheeks.

Holt Collier passed away in a nursing home in Greenville, Mississippi, at the age of 90. The familiar sight of this dignified man, with his iron-gray mustache, Vandyke beard and broad-brimmed hat walking the streets of his hometown, would be clearly missed.

Illustration 159. Holt Collier, famous bear hunter who was responsible for capturing the bear Roosevelt refused to shoot during his 1902 Mississippi bear hunt. *Courtesy Theodore Roosevelt Collection, Harvard College Library.*

Chapter Eleven

The Cartoon

In *The Campaign of '48 in Star Cartoons* (in which *The Star* presents the story of the 1948 election year [*Illustration 161*]), a vivid description of a cartoonist is featured:

"A cartoonist is many things to many men. To some he is a clown, tickling the world with the point of his pen. To others he is a wit, drafting cogent comment on the course of events, coming through on deadline with the day's perfectly incisive remark. To still others he is a sort of intellectual gadfly, stinging sinners to repentance with a barb of ridicule. But if he is true to himself he also is a reporter in the finest sense of the word, telling the story day by day with maximum economy, clarity and truth."

In 1926 Berryman declared in an address he delivered at the School of Journalism of the University of Missouri:

"There is nothing in our modern life so alarming as the power which reckless and dissolute talent has to make virtuous life seem provincial and ridiculous, vicious life graceful and metropolitan. The cartoonist's pencil cannot, however, defeat a good measure. Caricature is powerless against an administration that is honest and competent. Powerless against a public official who does his duty in his place."

For many years political cartoons have been used with great effect in European countries. The most famous and powerful cartoons expressing the political opinion were published in *Punch* in London. In America *Harper's* and *Leslie's* weeklies, *Punch* and *Judge*, were the most influential of all the weekly papers.

A political cartoonist must keep in step with the news as far as possible or be left behind. The theory that one picture is worth a thousand words gained support through the newspaper cartoons.

Clifford Berryman possessed prolific creative powers, and produced a cartoon a day for over 50 years.

His daughter, an art critic for *The Washington Evening Star*, was well aware of her gifted father's work. In a review of his exhibit at the Corcoran Gallery she wrote:

"Cartoons are a branch of art in which the transmission of ideas is paramount. This is currently demonstrated by the exhibition of original cartoons by Clifford K. Berryman now on view at the Corcoran Gallery of Art.

"The 'story-telling' aspect of pictures, so strongly condemned by modern artists, is the lifeblood of a cartoon. A drawing may be beautifully executed, may have decorative qualities, admirable composition and creative design, all of which will make it good art. But unless it

Illustration 160. Berryman illustrated the cover of *The Cartoon* magazine on April 11, 1908. Press of the World Pub. Co., Metropolitan Life Bldg., New York. *Courtesy Florence Berryman.*

presents an idea, forcefully and convincingly, it is not a good cartoon.

"The primary importance of ideas has always been stressed by Mr. Berryman. Many a boy in his teens aspiring to be a cartoonist, and in some cases having gotten a good start on his high school paper, has come to *The Star's* cartoonist for advice.

" 'Study history and politics,' Mr. Berryman invariably counsels. 'You would not be interested in a cartoonist's career if you didn't have some talent for drawing. It is much easier to develop that than it is to have something to say, every day for years, and your statement must be firmly based on knowledge.'

"The political cartoon, Mr. Berryman's specialty, has to make its impact in one blow, a requirement which gives it a character quite

The Campaign of '48
in
Star
CARTOONS

A publication of The Washington Star

Illustration 161. This cartoon appeared on the cover of *The Campaign of '48 in Star Cartoons* published by *The Washington Evening Star* in book form. The cartoons reproduced in the book first appeared on page one of *The Star*. Drawn by *The Star's* three cartoonists, Clifford Berryman, his son, Jim, and Gib Crockett, the cartoons portray the ten months leading up to election day. *Courtesy Library of Congress.*

different from the comic strip, which can build up its effect step by step. The cartoon presupposes on the part of the reader some knowledge of current events, and less frequently, of history and literature. The widespread popularity of the cartoon bears witness to the intelligence of a large proportion of newspaper readers...."

"So one returns to the original argument that a cartoon is a form of art inextricably tied up with ideas. Cartoons cannot be abstract or pure esthetics: they are of and for the people. And people of the future will be able to read in cartoons by Clifford Berryman and his contemporaries what the people of today are doing, and suffering and hoping."

Berryman, creative on his own, also drew from the works of other artists. In a day when almost every cartoonist had a mascot, he most notably used symbols created by Sir John Tenniel whose work appeared in weekly and monthly serials: the Eagle, the Russian Bear (*Illustrations 162* and *163*), the British Lion and the New Year.

The symbolism of Thomas Nast also was perpetu-

ated by Berryman: the GOP elephant, the Tammany tiger (*Illustration 165*), the "ragbaby" of inflation and, emblematic of labor, the cap and dinner pail.

The imaginative cartoonist hated to draw women, despite their prominence in Washington, even when such people as Princess Alice, Theodore Roosevelt's daughter, and First Lady Eleanor Roosevelt were in the news.

One exception was Frances Perkins, Secretary of Labor. Because she was the first woman to hold cabinet office, he found himself having to draw her continuously.

Naturally, he created much of his own symbolism: Miss Democracy was depicted as a giggling, befrilled spinster, with corkscrew-curls (*Illustration 164*); the District of Columbia was a stalwart man in 18th century dress and the Squash Center farmers were real-life rural characters who assembled around the stove in Berryman's father's country store in Kentucky. However, he is probably best known as the originator of his roguish little Teddy Bear that brought many a smile to a sober face.

Illustration 162. "Don't You Want To Come In And See Grandma's Veto?" Berryman depicted the Russian Bear in the fairy-tale scene of Little Red Riding Hood and the Big Bad Wolf. Original. *Judith Waddell Collection.*

Illustration 163. "So you're the Big Bad Bear!" November 7, 1933. *Courtesy Library of Congress.*

Illustration 164. "The great Democratic Handicap." Especially note in the spectator's box Berryman's own creation "Miss Democracy," depicted as a giggling, befrilled spinster with corkscrew curls. *Courtesy Smithsonian Institution.*

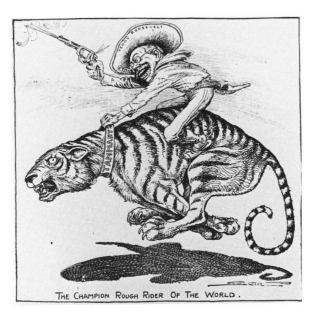

Illustration 165. "The Champion Rough Rider of the World," *The Evening Post* (Denver), from the book *A Cartoon History of Roosevelt's Career* by Albert Shaw, copyright 1910 by Review of Reviews Company. *Courtesy Toby Roberts.*

Illustration 166. "Rejoicing Over the End of the Hunt." The Bears: "We're glad he's gone." *The Tribune* (Minneapolis), from the book *A Cartoon History of Roosevelt's Career* by Albert Shaw, copyright 1910 by the Review of Reviews Company. *Courtesy Toby Roberts.*

Illustration 167. This self-portrait of Clifford Berryman depicts the ten Chief Executives of the United States he had known. The Presidents are (in order) Benjamin Harrison, Cleveland, McKinley, Theodore Roosevelt, Taft, Wilson, Harding, Coolidge, Hoover and Franklin D. Roosevelt, and, of course, not to be forgotten, his famous little Teddy Bear inquisitively peeking over the drawing board. *The Evening Star*, July 4, 1943. *Courtesy Library of Congress.*

Illustration 168. "Thinking of what may be," 1912 to 1914. Original. *Courtesy Library of Congress.*

Illustration 169. "Uncle Sam Would Not That Role Be More Becoming To." Original. *Courtesy The Smithsonian Institution.*

Illustration 170. "Recreating Rapidan River." Original. *Courtesy Betty Ruth Austin (Clifford Berryman's niece).*

Illustration 171. "It May Yet Come To This!" Original. *Courtesy Dr. and Mrs. Allen Mathies.*

Illustration 172. "The Big Stick In The Caribbean Sea," *The Herald* (New York), from the book *A Cartoon History of Roosevelt's Career* by Albert Shaw, copyright 1910 by Review of Reviews Company. *Courtesy Toby Roberts.*

Illustration 173. "' A Grizzly Path: President Roosevelt and the Trusts. President Roosevelt: 'Is it safe to shoot? The Bear: 'Does he mean business?' " *Westminster Budget* (London), from the book *A Cartoon History of Roosevelt's Career* by Albert Shaw, copyright 1910 by the Review of Reviews Company. *Courtesy Toby Roberts.*

Chapter Twelve

Mrs. Berryman and Her Testimonial at Her Husband's 80th Birthday Party

Illustration 174. This large painting of Kate Berryman predominantly hangs in the Berryman home in Washington, D.C. *Courtesy Florence Berryman.*

At the time of his golden wedding anniversary observance, Clifford Berryman made this statement about his wife: "She has been a wonderful companion — and my worst critic. I listen to her criticisms, too. She has been a real guide — probably kept me out of lots of trouble."

Kate Berryman, a fifth-generation Washington resident, was a member of many societies. She felt very strongly about the importance of women in world history. It was one of her favorite themes at various women's clubs.

Her hobby was collecting antiques. Her family knew Kate Berryman to have a shrewd eye for a bargain. This hobby, however, was not shared by her husband. He disliked clutter and was much happier playing golf and going to a baseball game. Mrs. Berryman said she could tell by the way her husband put his key in the door whether the Washington Senators had won or lost.

Mrs. Berryman became an accomplished hostess. Photographs were not so readily available as they are today, so Clifford Berryman drew his cartoons after seeing public figures in person. Therefore, the couple frequently gave dinner parties for members of Congress and the Cabinet. Mrs. Berryman played hostess at these affairs.

Just eight months before he died, on his 80th birthday, Clifford Berryman was guest of honor at the Chevy Chase Club. Many of his cartoon subjects attended. This distinguished-looking veteran cartoonist was showered with congratulations from those present and thousands of others who, regretfully, were unable to attend.

Mrs. Berryman, as the sole exception to this so-called "stag" affair, outshone all other congratulations and tributes in her toast:

"Two days ago — Jim told me I might be called on to make a few remarks, at this marvelous tribute to Cliff. So I got mentally busy trying to assemble some of the memories of the past, which of course must be an expose of personalities and sentiment. We Southerners don't mind showing our emotions — we are like that.

"When I left home I thought I knew these few remarks by heart, but since coming here and looking into your faces, and realizing what top-notchers you all are, I'm now scared to death and I am afraid I'll have to read from my notes.

"First of all, I want to thank my three hosts, Mr. Kauffmann, Mr. McKelway and Jim Berryman, for including me in this most exclusive audience. The events of this evening will be a cherished memory to me, as long as life lasts, and who knows? I may remember it long after I have vanished into the dimness of the Great Beyond.

"For over 60 years I have watched Cliff Berryman develop from a normal country boy into the resourceful gentleman he is today. For 56 years we have walked along life's pathway. Ours has been a long, full, rich, eventful and congenial life together, and I'm reminded of John Masefield (Jim's favorite poet) who said, 'Just to sit by him and hold his hand is wealth, surpassing all minted treasure.' Of course on life's pathway one meets with many problems, most of which we can solve; but there are some, which we cannot answer, until we arrive in another sphere. For instance, most of you, I'm sure, have gone out into a clear, cold, crisp winter night and looked up at those little specs in the cobalt beyond, and they seemed so near you felt that you could easily pick a handful. But they made you mad, too, because they winked at you and seemed to say, 'I know something, and I won't tell you'; so we will have to find out in the distant future, the SECRETS of the STARS, and the MIRACLE of BIRTH, and the MYSTERY of SLEEP, but there is ONE thing I do know, NOW — and that is, I know the Fairies danced upon the hearth the night Cliff was born and they brought him many gifts. I know that hearth well. I've sat there many times and enjoyed its warmth and its glow. That hearth was the kind you read about in song and story: It was in an old Colonial house, on a 2,000-acre farm, on the Kentucky River.

"Cliff was number ten of the third generation of Berryman babies who had played on that hearth. The Fairies had prepared a marvelous background for Cliff — A BACKGROUND of patriotic, cultured and God-fearing forebears and they chose two fine people to be his parents.

"Among the other gifts they brought him, was PERFECT HEALTH, a happy DISPOSITION, the gift of LAUGHTER, and they put into his HEART the milk of HUMAN KINDNESS, and they placed him in TUNE with the INFINITE. I know you will all acknowledge they gave him PERSONAL PULCHRITUDE. They gave him great talent, they made him a GENIUS and to top it all, they gave him that rare gift of LIFELONG FRIENDSHIP, evidenced here tonight by your presence. I love you all for coming to honor Cliff, and so let us drink another toast to him, in the language of Omar the Tentmaker, who said, 'Come, my dears, fill up the cup with cheer, and let us drink — just today, with no past regrets, nor future fears. For tomorrow? Why, tomorrow, I, myself, may be with yesterday's 7,000 years.' I thank you."

Chapter Thirteen

The Children of Clifford K. Berryman

Clifford Berryman and his wife, Kate, started their family in Washington soon after they were married in 1893.

Their first child, Mary Belle, died of polio when only 14 months old. This tragic loss left an emptiness in the Berryman's home and hearts until their second little girl, Florence Seville, was born on September 10, 1900. The bright, pretty child grew into a vivacious, ambitious young woman. She loved to play the piano and dreamed of becoming a concert pianist, but misfortune struck the Berryman family once again.

When Florence was 20, she developed scarlet fever. The talented pianist whose life was full of the sound of music was left completely deaf.

Inheriting her father's determination and love of life, Florence went on to become an excellent art critic for *The Washington Evening Star*. In addition, she lectured and wrote articles for fine art magazines.

I had the pleasure of meeting Florence Berryman (*Illustration 176*) in the fall of 1986. The delightful, witty lady, now retired and in her 80s, still resides in the Berryman home that her father purchased in 1939 (*Illustration 175*). The charming three-story brick house is of the style typically built in Washington in those early days. Inside the house the walls are lined with huge paintings of Florence's ancestors.

As did her father, Florence really enjoys people. A member of several prestigious Washington clubs and associations, this gregarious lady still leads a very active social life. She took great pleasure in sharing stories of her father with me.

Clifford Berryman was a devoted father. Florence laughingly told how she looked forward to her weekly treat of going to the nickel movies. Her voice filled with affection as she proudly told of the important engagements her father would turn down before he would miss taking her on this favorite outing.

Although her father disliked hunting and did not share his wife's love of collecting, his relationship with bears inspired friends and admirers to fill his house with bear related gifts.

Florence recalls as a child, a stuffed, real bear cub that greeted guests as they entered their home. The appealing little cub held a tray to receive calling cards (decorative business cards), a popular custom in the early 1900s.

Florence also inherited her father's generosity. She presented a large percentage of her father's original drawings and his collection of books, correspondence and manuscripts for permanent placement at the Library of Congress to be preserved, treasured and enjoyed by visitors in the years to come.

In an article Florence Berryman wrote about her father she said:

"The fact that my father was a 'prophet honored even in his own land' was a source of the deepest and most abiding satisfaction to him. The affection and esteem of the people who knew him best, and with whom he was most closely associated seemed to have larger dimensions for him than equivalent honors from farther away."

James Thomas (*Illustrations 177* and *178*) was the Berryman's only son and last child. He was born June 8, 1902, the same year in which Clifford drew his famous Berryman Bear. It has been said one reason Berryman did not copyright this idea was because of the happiness and pride he was feeling from the birth of his heir.

The kind, gentle cartoonist said his reward was knowing he had inspired the creation of the Teddy Bear toy that had made millions of children happy.

One of Berryman's greatest satisfactions was that his son had not only inherited his own great talent, but had chosen to follow in his footsteps as a cartoonist. Jim (as his friends called him) joined *The Washington Evening Star* in 1924. Then two years later he married Louise Marble Rhys. They had one son, Rhys Morgan.

By the time James was 29 he had become editorial illustrator and three years later he became *The Washington Evening Star* and *Sporting News* sports cartoonist.

Jim began collaborating with his father on the front page political cartoons in 1941. Unlike his father, who drew in pen and ink, James varied his cartoons with crayon, pencil and brush work, but his style resembled that of his father to such a remarkable degree that when the Berrymans began taking turns in pictorially commentating on *The Evening Star*'s front page, many subscribers did not notice the difference. Only by scrutinizing the signatures could they tell. The son signed his name Jim Berryman whereas his father used, simply, Berryman. However, the only time Jim drew the popular Berryman Bear was when he cartooned his father. (*Illustration 26*).

Jim was the "apple of his father's twinkling eye." No compliments pleased Clifford more than the ones he frequently received for his son's drawings. He felt Jim's artistic ability was far superior to his. He has proudly stated about his son: "He has had lessons, he is a superior draftsman and can portray action."

As the senior Berryman's output became reduced, Jim continued to be his understudy, relieving him of the sole responsibility. With his father's death in 1949, Jim succeeded him as *The Washington Evening Star*'s political cartoonist. He also shared with his father the prestigious distinction of being awarded the Pulitzer Prize. On May 1, 1950, his cartoon, "All Set for a Super-Secret Session in Washington" was selected for this honor.

James Berryman passed away at the age of 60. At this writing his son, Rhys, now in his mid 40s, has no children, so therefore, there is no heir to carry on the famous Berryman name.

Illustration 175. Here I am standing in front of the charming Berryman home in Washington, D.C., where Clifford Berryman lived from 1939 until his death in 1949. It was here I met his daughter, Florence, who still lives in the home full of wonderful memories of her beloved father.

Illustration 176. Florence Berryman (Clifford Berryman's daughter) expresses her delight when I gave her a Teddy Bear when we met for the first time in September 1986.

Illustration 177. Photograph of Clifford Berryman taken in 1910 with his son, James, then 8, and his beautiful daughter, Florence, age 10. *Courtesy Florence Berryman.*

Illustration 178. James Berryman (Clifford Berryman's son) watches with endless admiration as his father sketches. Unlike James who varied his cartoons with crayon, pencil and brush, his father worked solely in pen and ink. *Copyright* The Washington Post, *reprinted by permission of the D.C. Public Library.*

Chapter Fourteen

The Clifford Berryman Teddy Bear

While working on the manuscript for this book I developed a deep admiration for Clifford Berryman, and a sincere love of his little cartoon bear that earned the reputation of representing all that was good in the world.

Then one day I was sentimentally looking at my favorite cartoon *(Illustration 79)*, when suddenly I thought how wonderful it would be to make an actual Clifford Berryman Teddy Bear — an endearing little bruin that would keep the memory of Berryman's famous cartoon creation alive forever.

So I got busy, and with the help of my dear friend, Flore Emory, we designed a prototype bear.

Excitedly I journeyed to Germany to present my idea to the prestigious company of Margarete Steiff GmBH. After discussing my proposal with Dr. Herbert Zimmermann, the president of the company, and Jörg Jünginger, the chief designer, I was overjoyed when Dr. Zimmermann agreed to manufacture the Clifford Berryman Bear.

Illustration 179. I was proud to have my Clifford Berryman Teddy Bear manufactured by the prestigious company of Margarete Steiff GmBH.

Illustration 180. Like Berryman's famous little cartoon bear, the Clifford Berryman Teddy Bear is lovable and mischievous.

Illustration 181. This cartoon Berryman drew of his bear saying "Good Night! You've had quite enough!" would seem appropriate and may well have been used for the closing cartoon of one of his famous "Chalk Talks." *Courtesy Library of Congress.*

Bibliography

Books

Bialosky, Peggy & Alan, *The Teddy Bear Catalog*, Workman Publishing, New York, 1980.

Fraley, Tobin, *The Carousel Animal*, Zephyr Press, Berkeley, California.

Greenhouse, Bernard L., *Political Postcards 1900-1980 A Price Guide*, Postcard Press, New York, 1984.

Hake, Theodore L., *Political Buttons Book III 1789-1916*, Americana and Collectibles Press, York, Pennsylvania, 1978.

Hutchings, Margaret, *Teddy Bears and How to Make Them*. New York: Dover Publications, 1964.

Lewis, Wm. Draper, *The Life of Theodore Roosevelt*, The United Publishers, United States, 1919.

McClung, Robert M., *The Mighty Bears*, Random House, New York, 1967.

Nicholson, Susan Brown, *Teddy Bears On Paper*, Taylor Publishing, Dallas, Texas, 1985.

Rawick, George P. (general editor), Jan Hillegas, Ken Lawrence, (editors), *"The American Slave: A Composite Autobiography,"* Supplement, Series 1, Volume 7, Greenwood Press, Westport, Connecticut, London, England, 1978.

Russell, Thomas H., *Life and Work of Theodore Roosevelt*, 1919.

Roosevelt, Theodore, *Theodore Roosevelt's Letters to His Children*, Charles Scribner's Sons, New York, 1919.

Roosevelt, Theodore, *Cowboys and Kings, Three Great Letters*, Harvard University Press, Cambridge, 1954.

Roosevelt, Theodore, *African Game Trails*, Syndicate Publishing Company, New York, London, 1909, 1910.

Schoonmaker, Patricia N., *The Collector's History of the Teddy Bear*, Hobby House Press, Cumberland, Maryland, 1981.

Shaw, Albert, *A Cartoon History of Roosevelt's Career*, The Review of Reviews Company, New York, 1910.

Waring, Philippa and Peter, *In Praise of Teddy Bears*, Caledonian Graphics Ltd., Great Britain, 1980.

The Washington Star, *The Campaign of '48 in Star Cartoons*, Washington, D.C., 1948.

Journals

Corcoran Chronicle, The Corcoran Gallery of Art, Volume 1, Number 1, Washington, D.C., 1984.

Student Illustrator, Volume 1. Washington, D.C., 1916.

Quarterly Journal of Current Acquisitions, Washington, D.C., Library of Congress, Volume 3, Number 2, February, 1946.

Articles

Baird, Joseph H., *The Evening Star*, June 3, 1943.

Bauman, Richard, "When Teddy Nearly Ruined Christmas," *Fedco Reporter*, December 1986.

Dickenson, Jacob M., "Stories and Reminiscences," *Outdoor America*, April 24, 1924.

Gable, John A. PhD., "The Many Sided Father of the Teddy Bear," *Bear Tracks*, Fall 1982.

Harris, Rev. Frederick Brown, "Unstained and Unashamed," *The Evening Star*, December 18, 1949.

Herald Bureau, "Christmas Jokers Send Toy Bears To President," *New York Herald*, December 28, 1902.

Lincoln, Norman G., "The Father of the Teddy Bear," *The Teddy Bear and friends®*, Hobby House Press, Inc., Summer 1985.

Morhart, Fred, "Luncheon and Prize to Clifford Berryman Mark His Fresh Triumphs," *The Goldfish Bowl*, National Press Club, Mid Summer 1944.

Port, Beverly, "Let's Talk Teddy Bears," *The Teddy Bear and friends®*, Hobby House Press, Inc., Fall 1987.

Roosevelt, Theodore, "The 1900's In The Louisiana Canebrakes," *Scribner's Magazine*, January 1908.

Schoonmaker, Patricia N., "Billie Possum," *The Teddy Bear and friends®*, Hobby House Press, Inc., Fall 1983.

Schreckinger, Sy, "The Teddy Bear Bank," *Antique Toy World*, December 1986.

Wilson, Gregory C., "How Teddy Bear Got His Name," *The Washington Post*, Potomac, November 30, 1969.

Woodford Sunday Newspaper, "Cartoonist Berryman Comes Today to Visit His Birthplace," April 23, 1939.

Press Release

Mendelsohn, Ink, "A Bull Market for Teddy Bears," *Smithsonian News Service*, December 1982.

Locations of Clifford K. Berryman's Cartoon Collections

Library of Congress, Washington, D.C.
Corcoran Gallery of Art, Washington, D.C.
British Museum
Folger Shakespeare Library
Franklin D. Roosevelt Library
Henry E. Huntington Library and Art Gallery, San
　　Marino, California

United States Supreme Court
University of Idaho
University of Missouri
University of Texas

As well as numerous clubs and public offices.

Index

(Numbers in bold refer to illustration numbers.)